ANIMAL MANDALAS COLORING BOOK FOR ADULTS

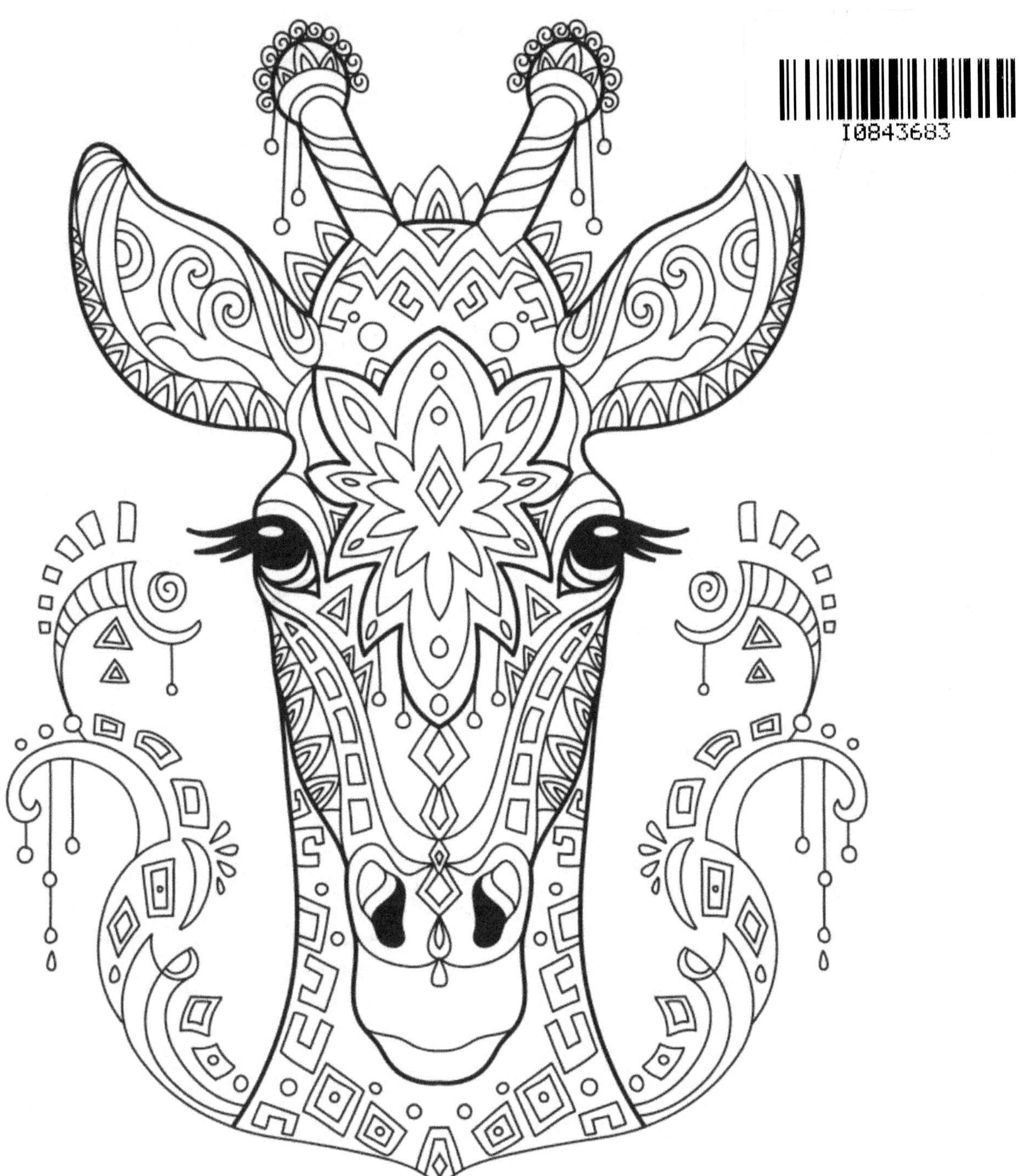

THIS BOOK BELONGS TO

....

....

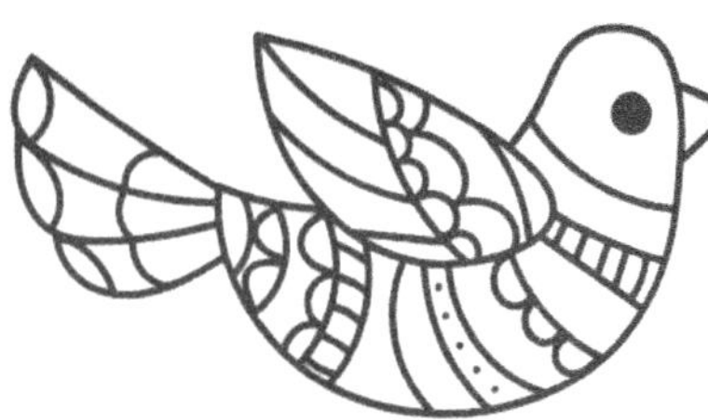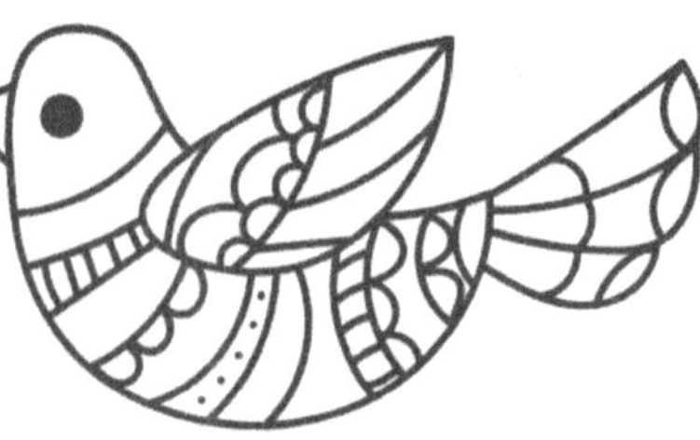

COLOR TEST PAGES

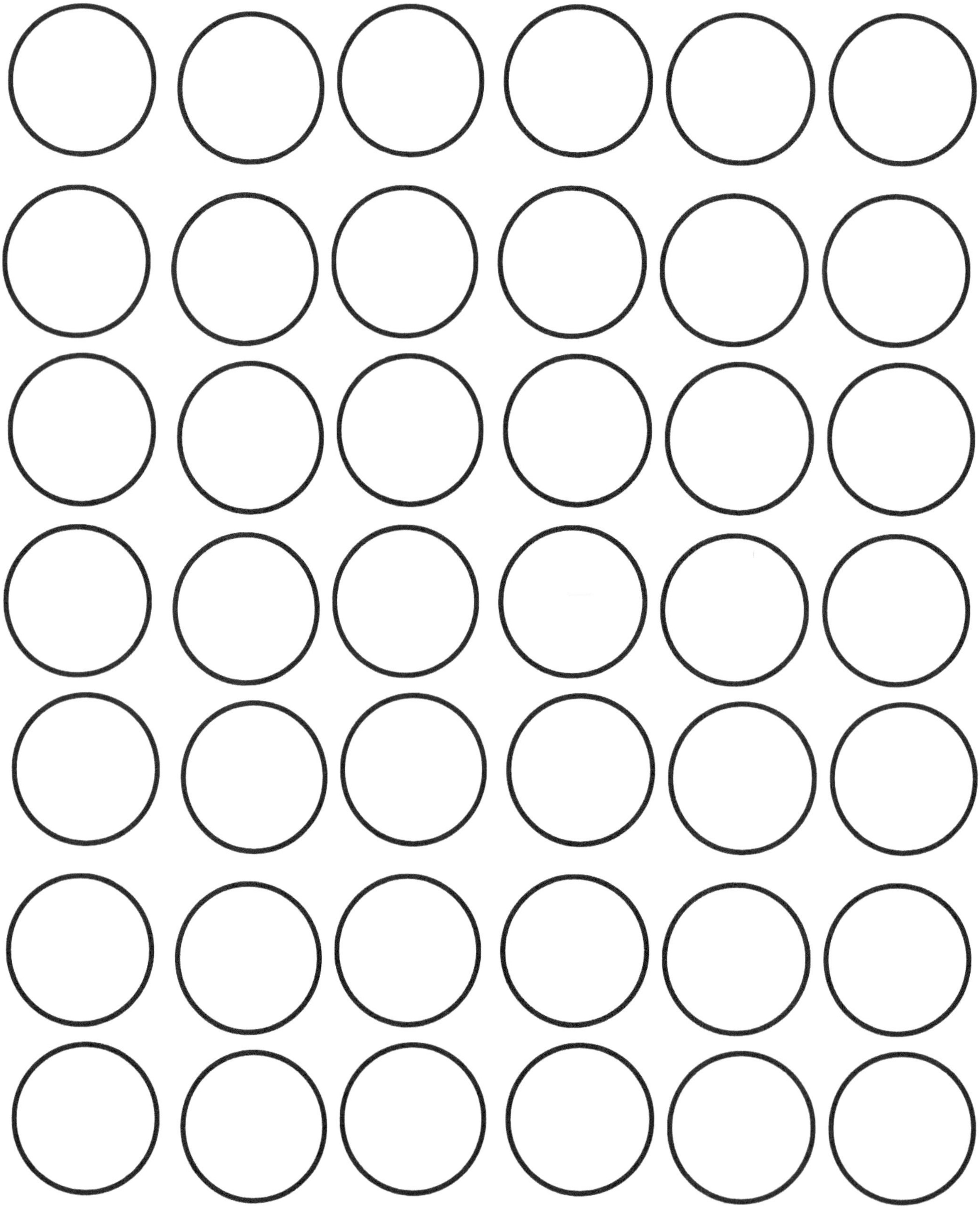

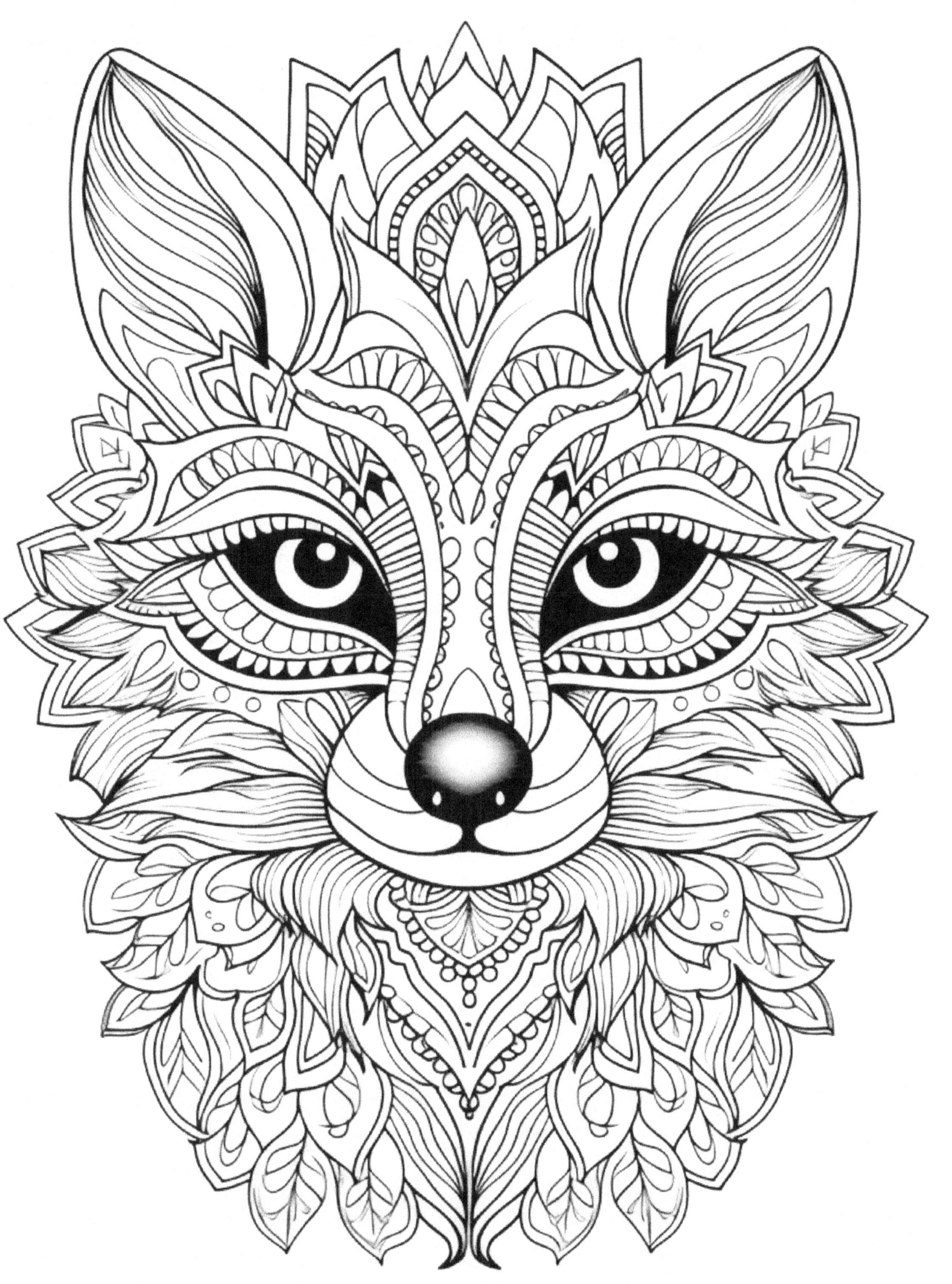

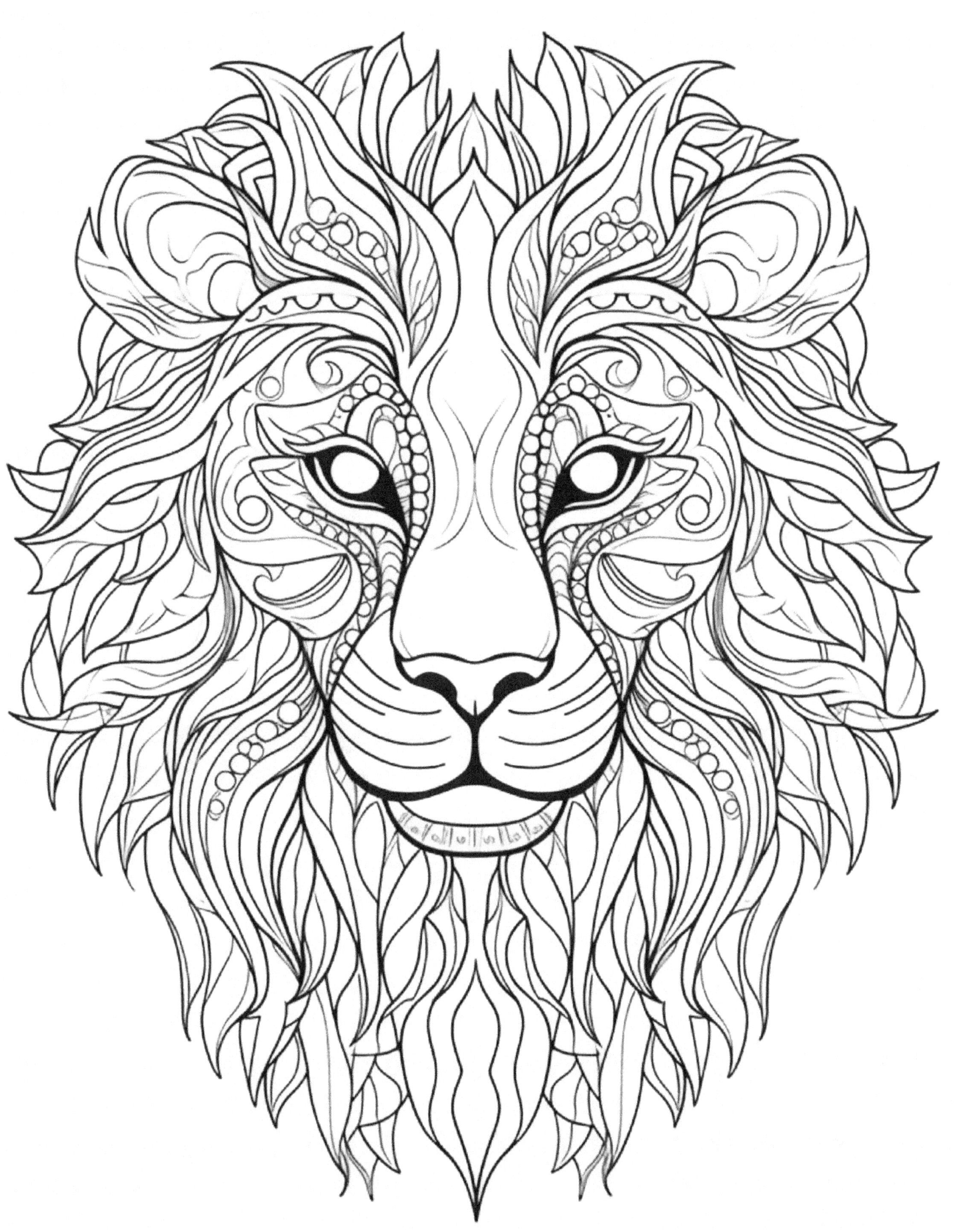

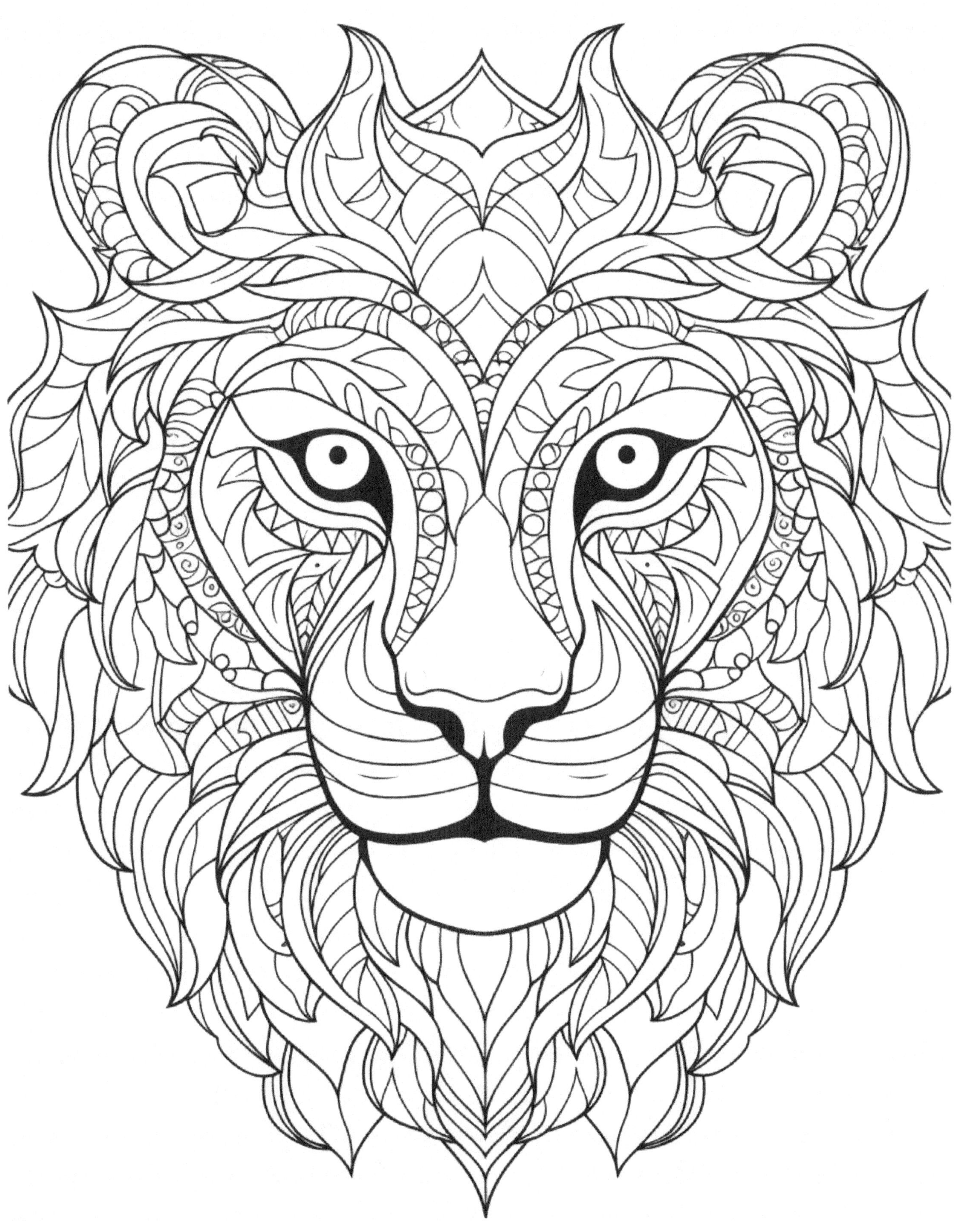

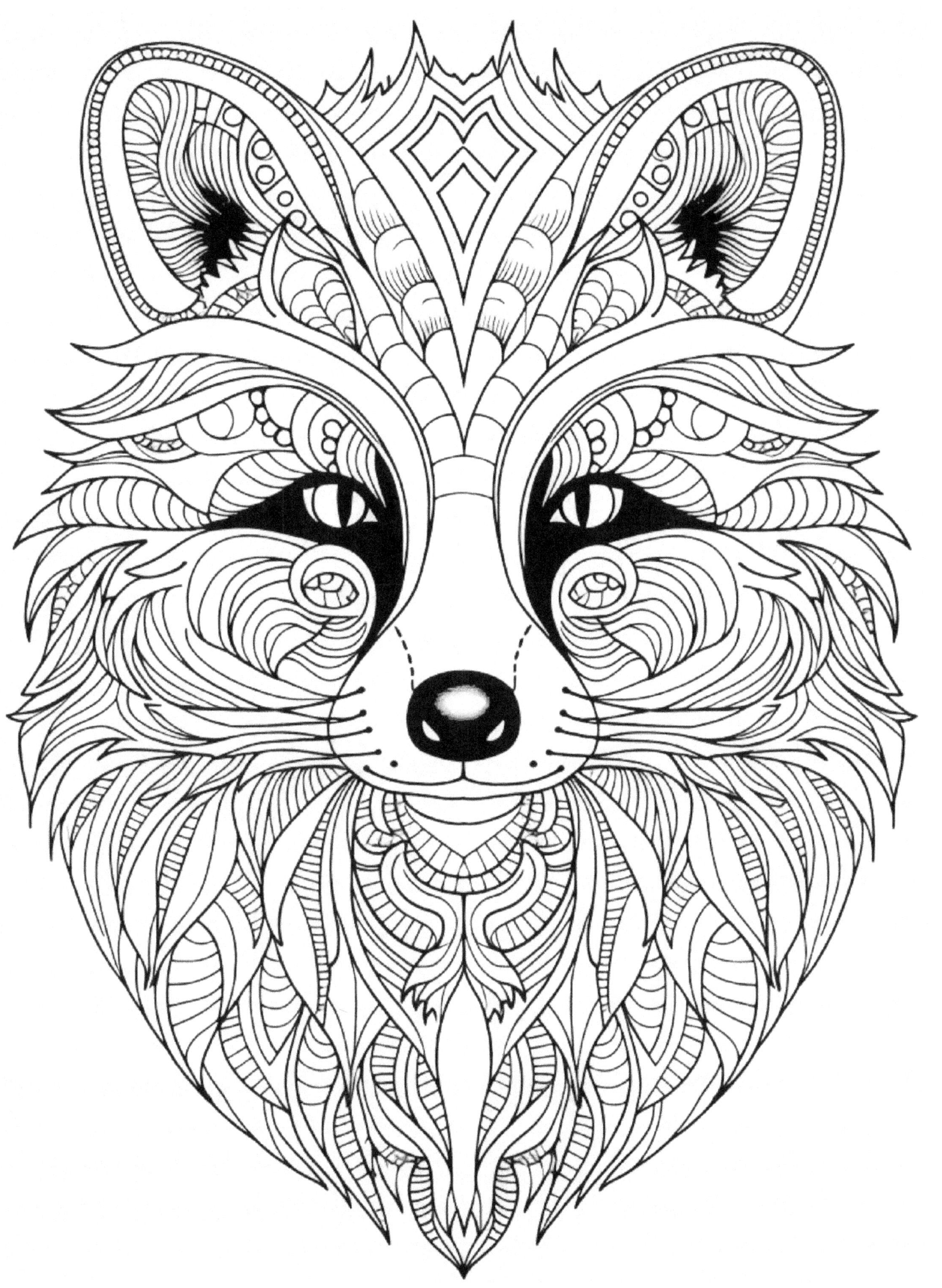

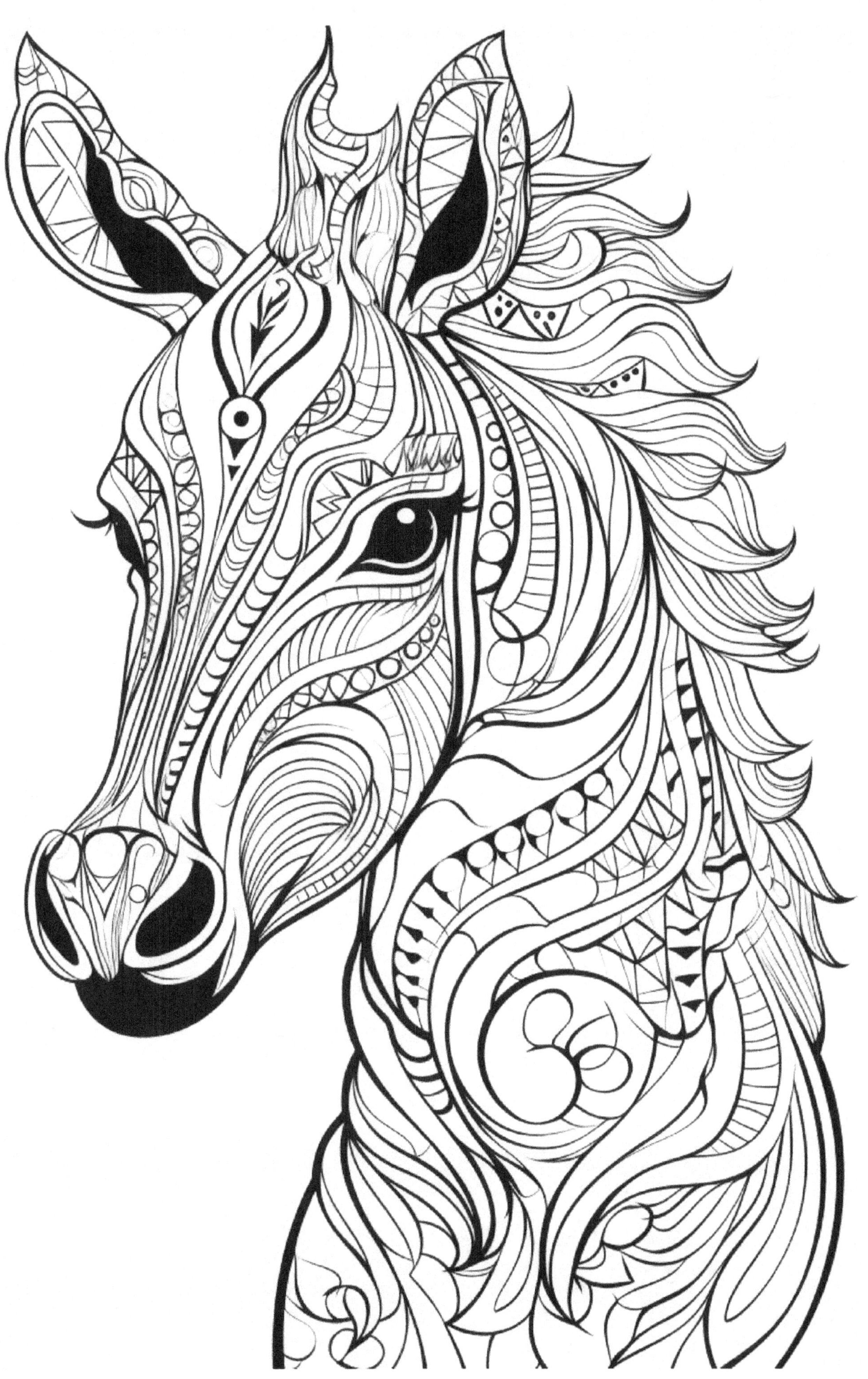

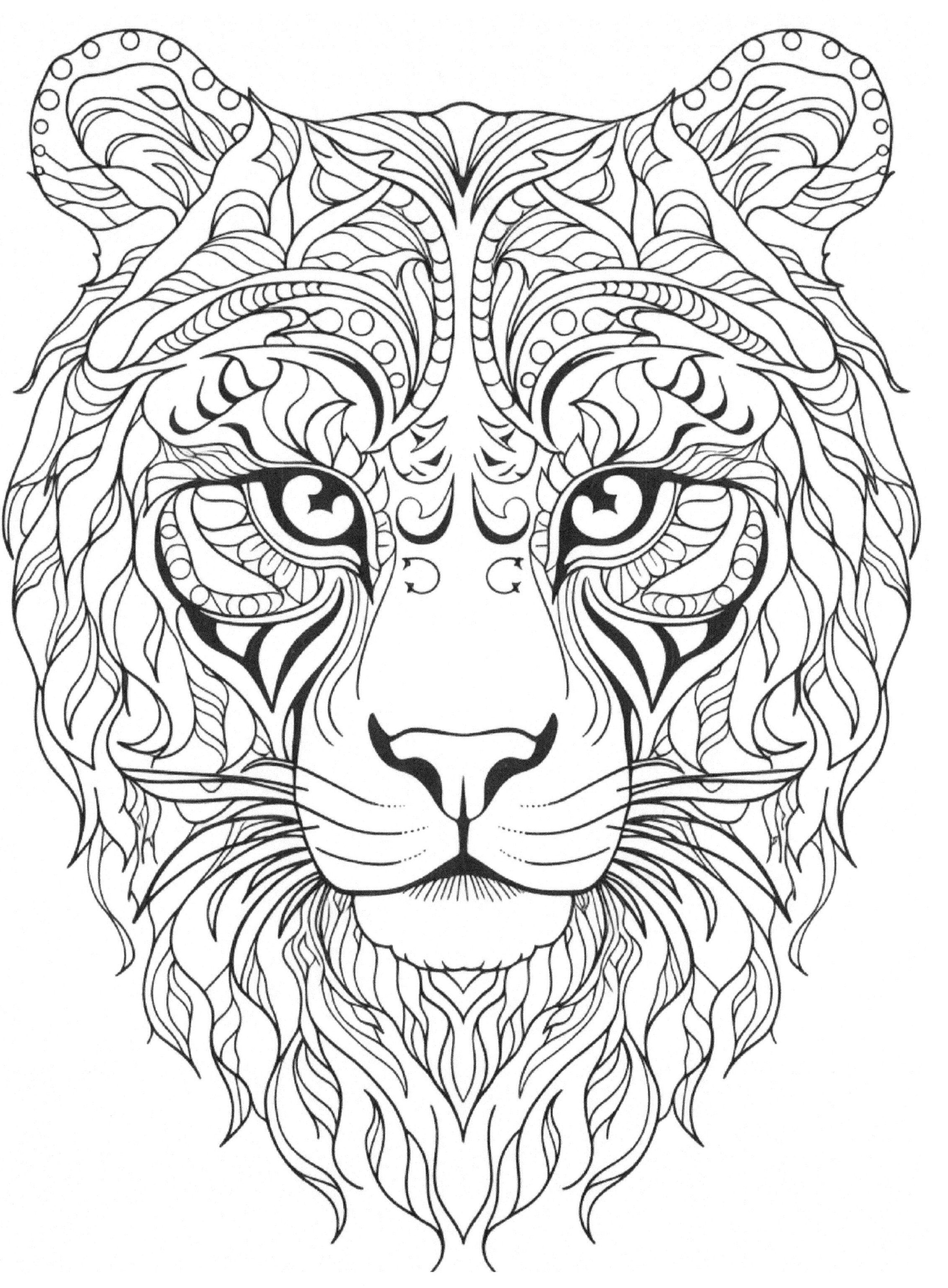

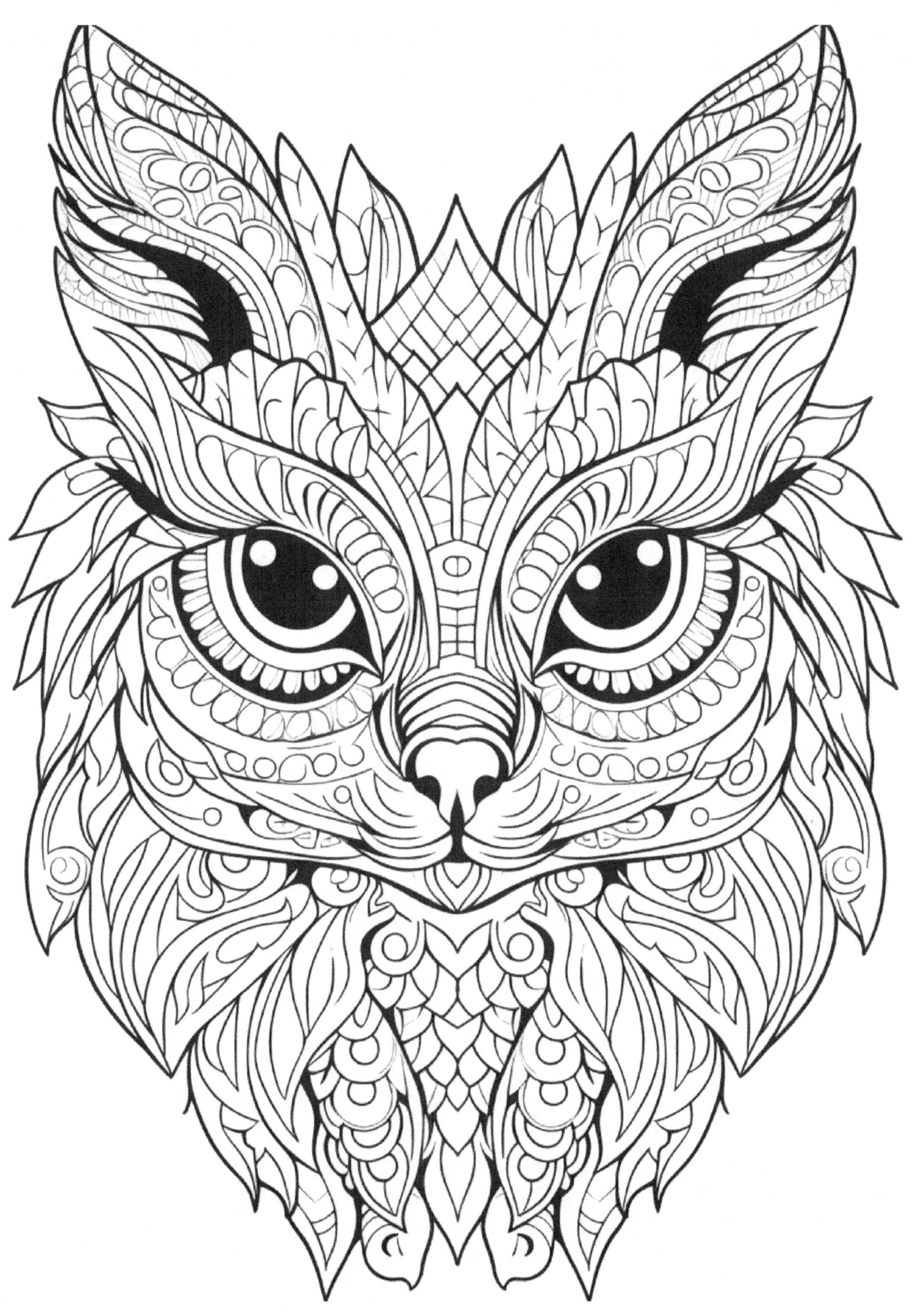

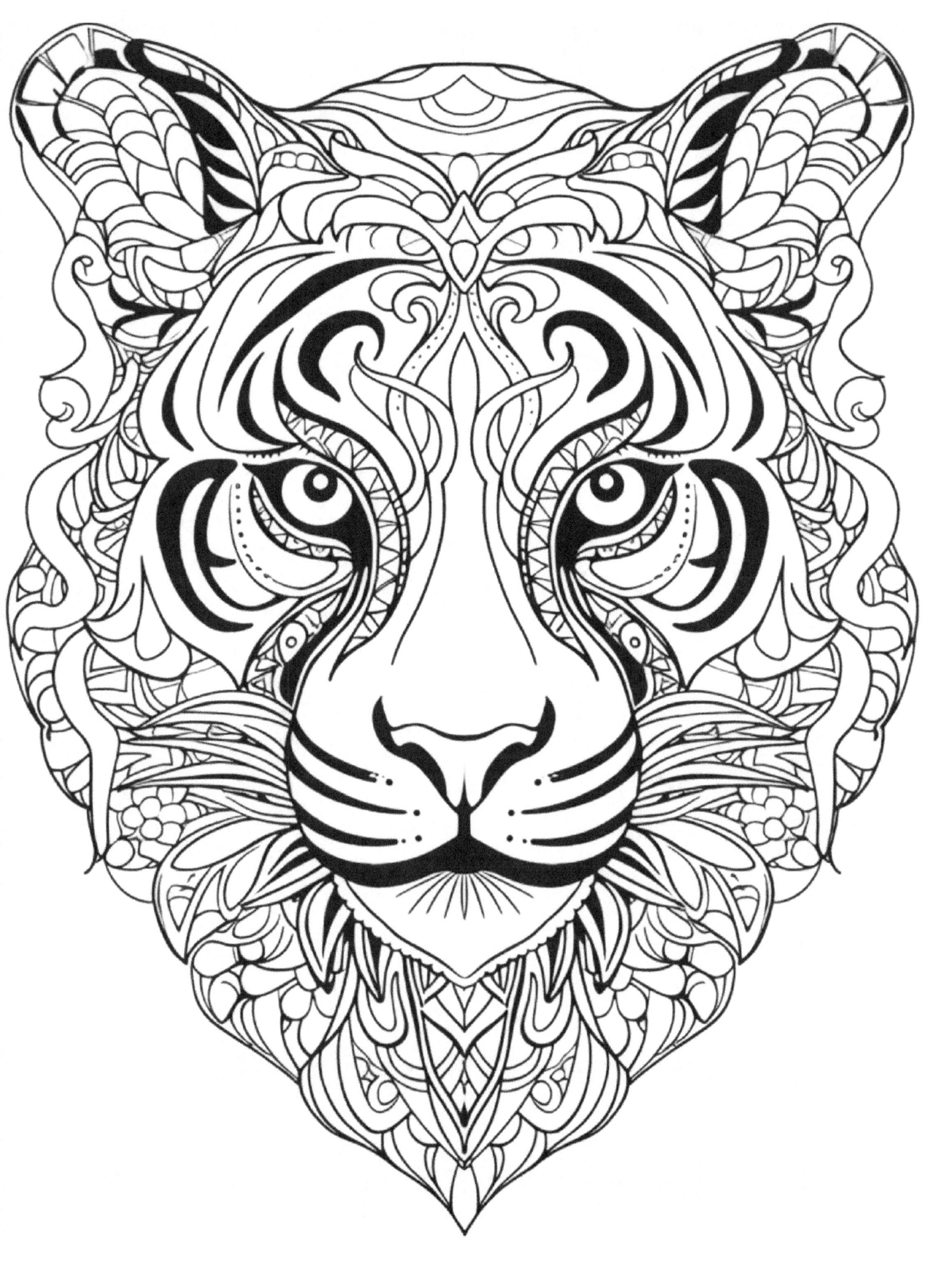

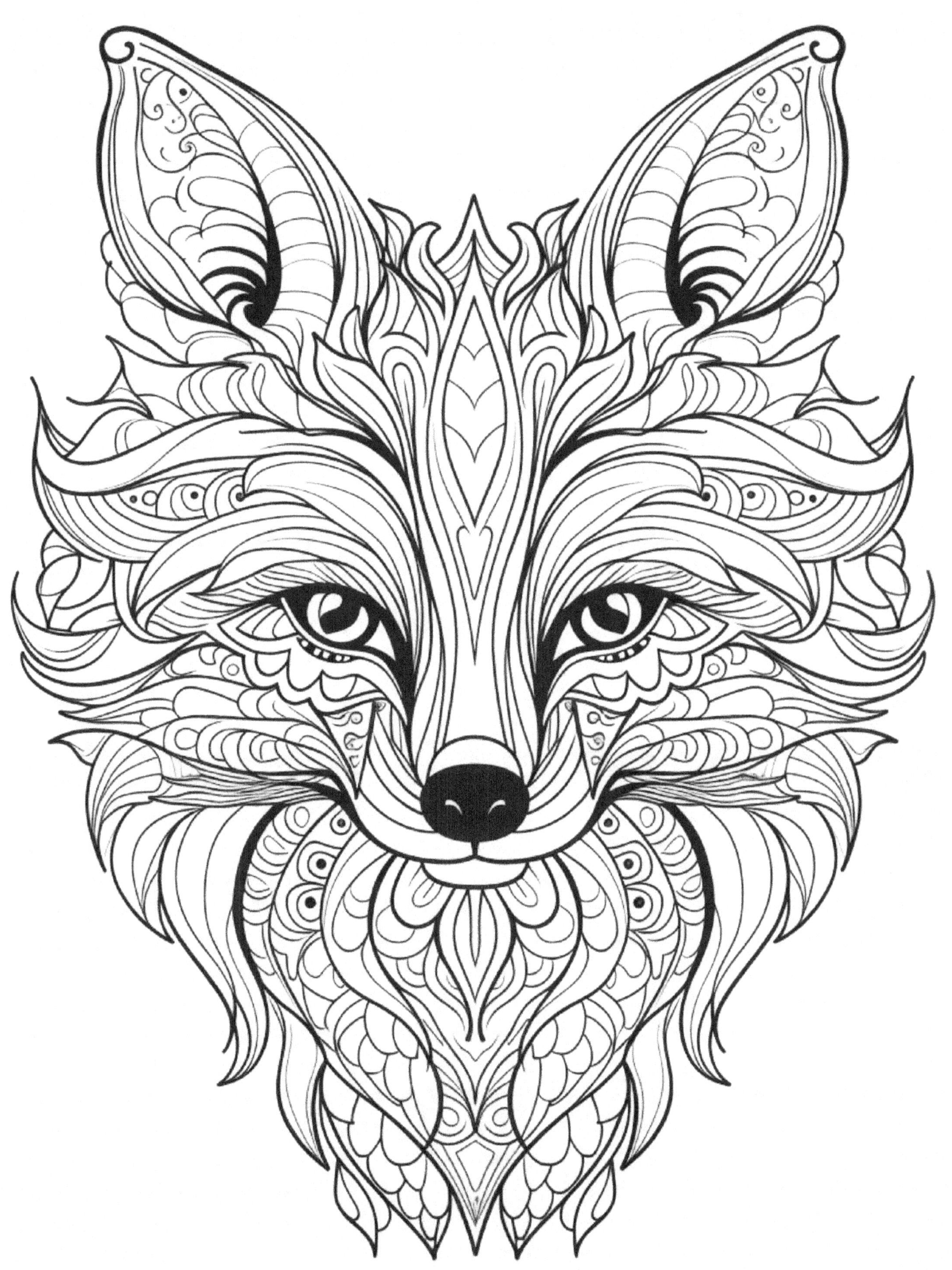

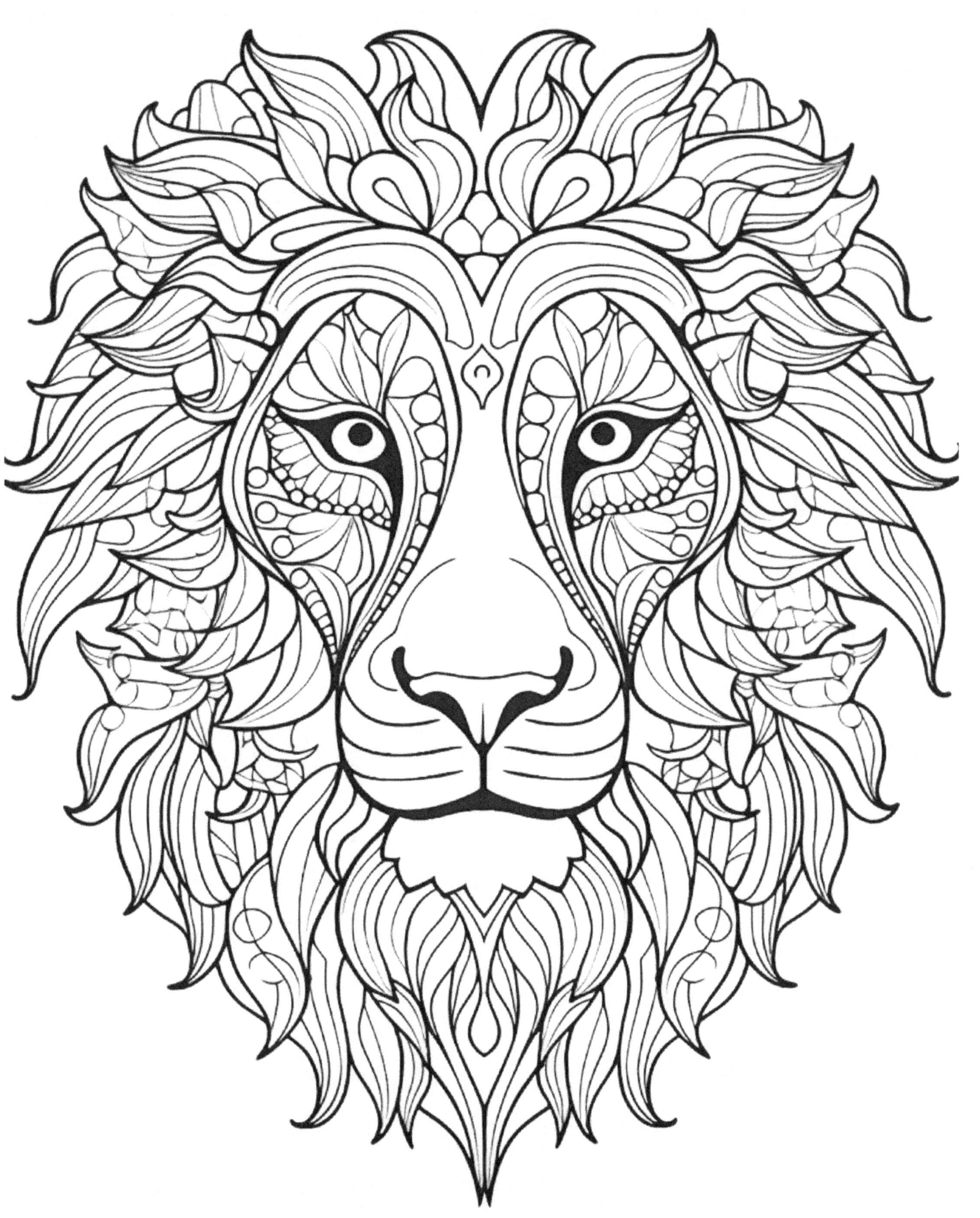

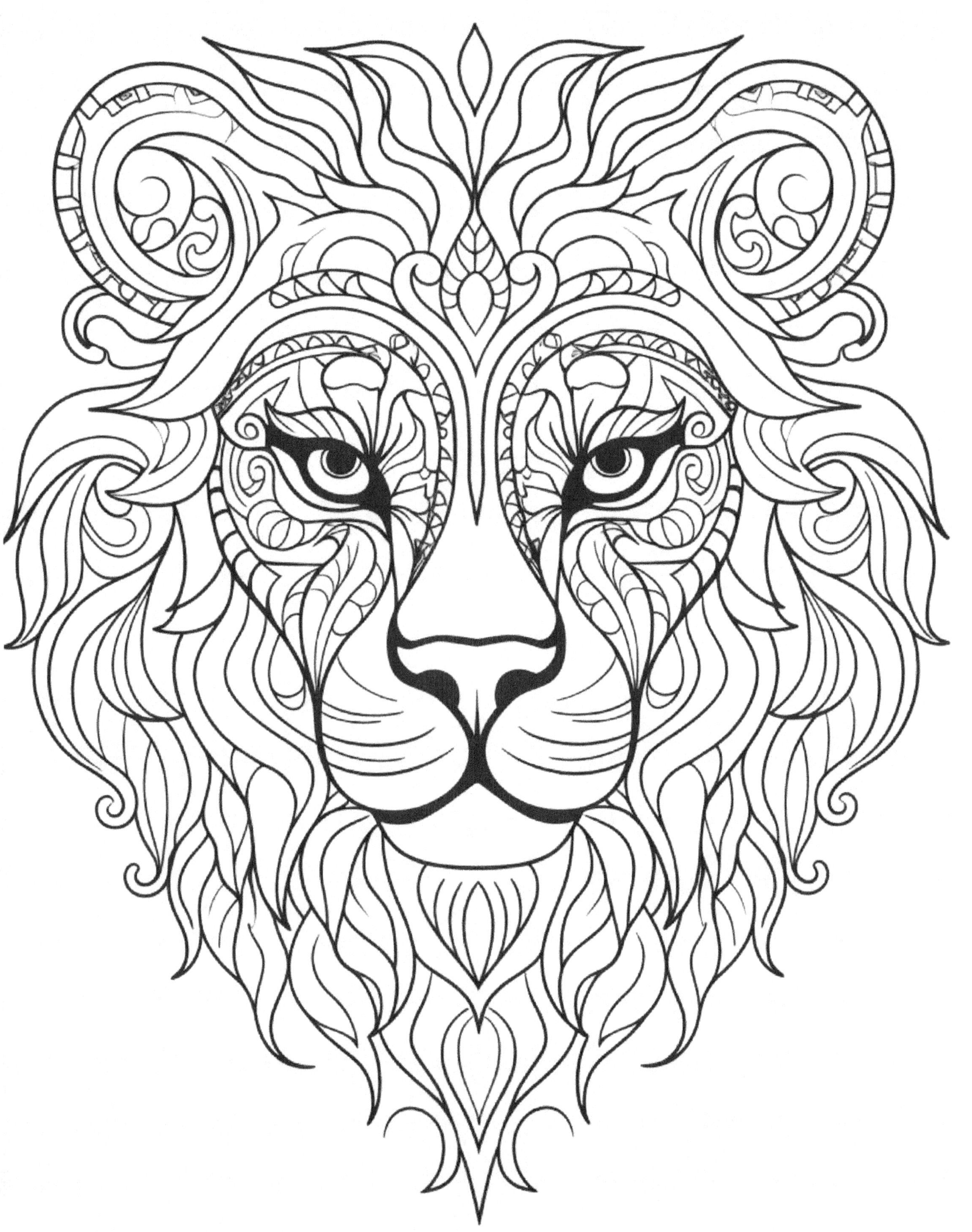

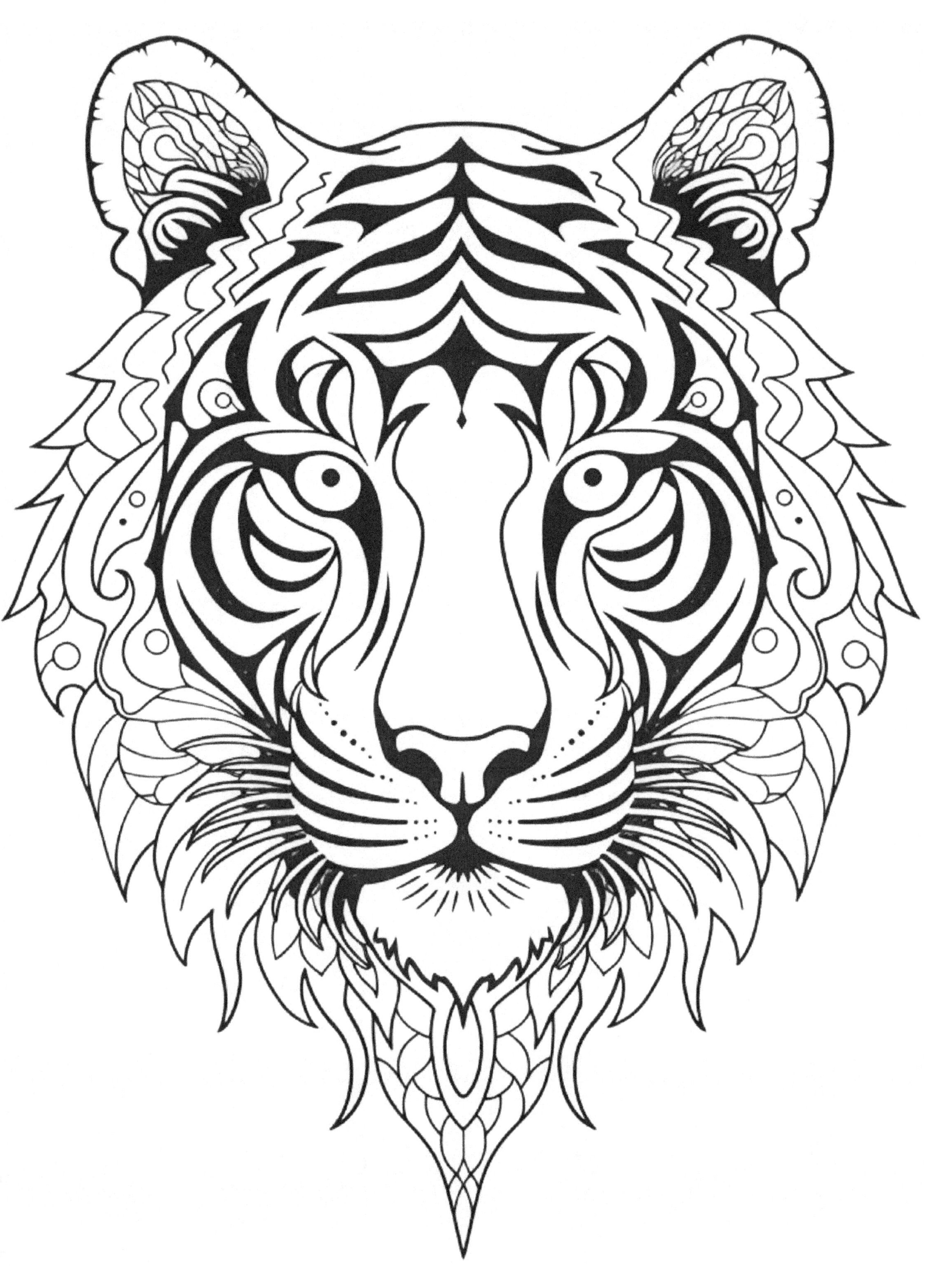

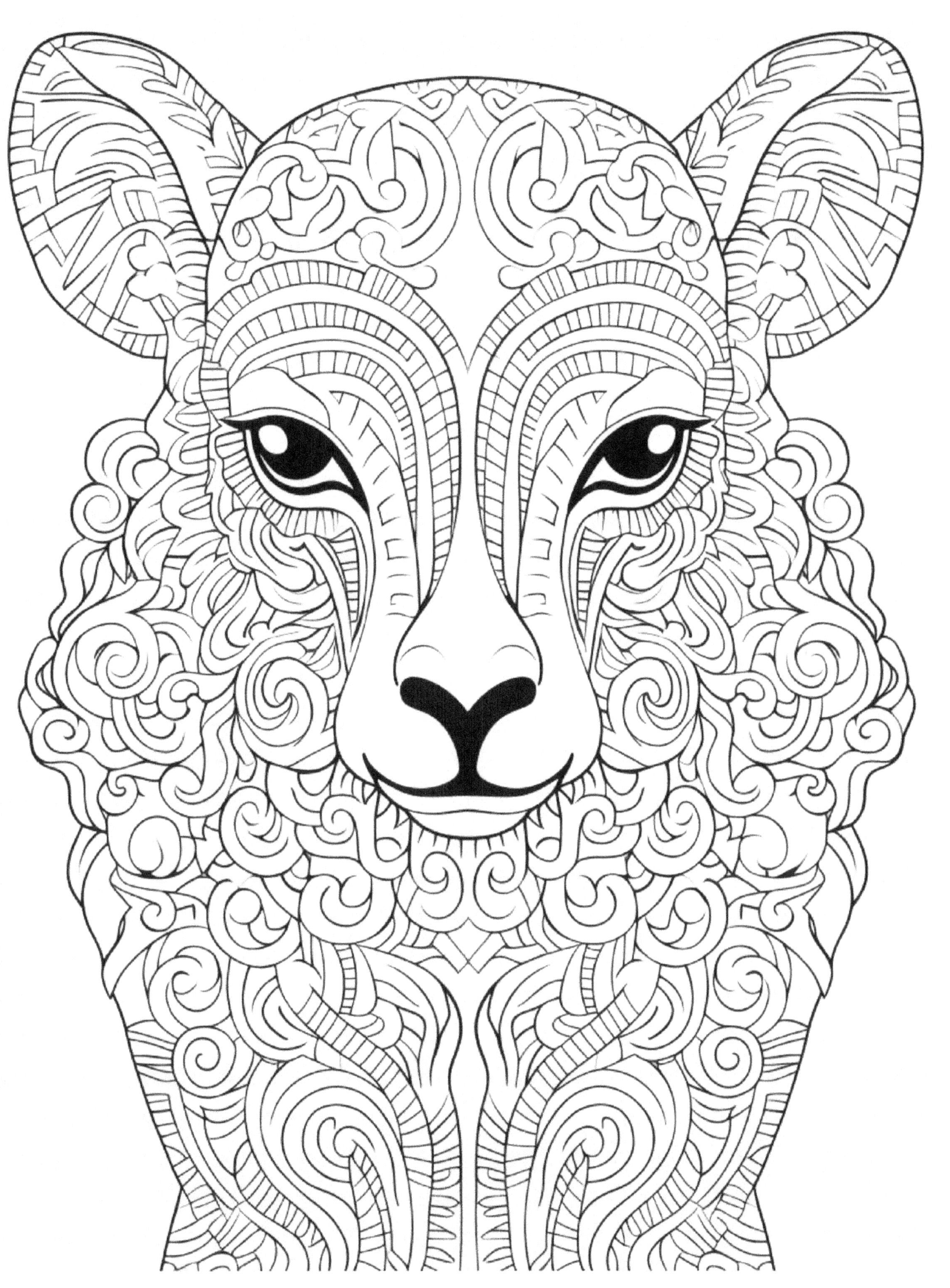

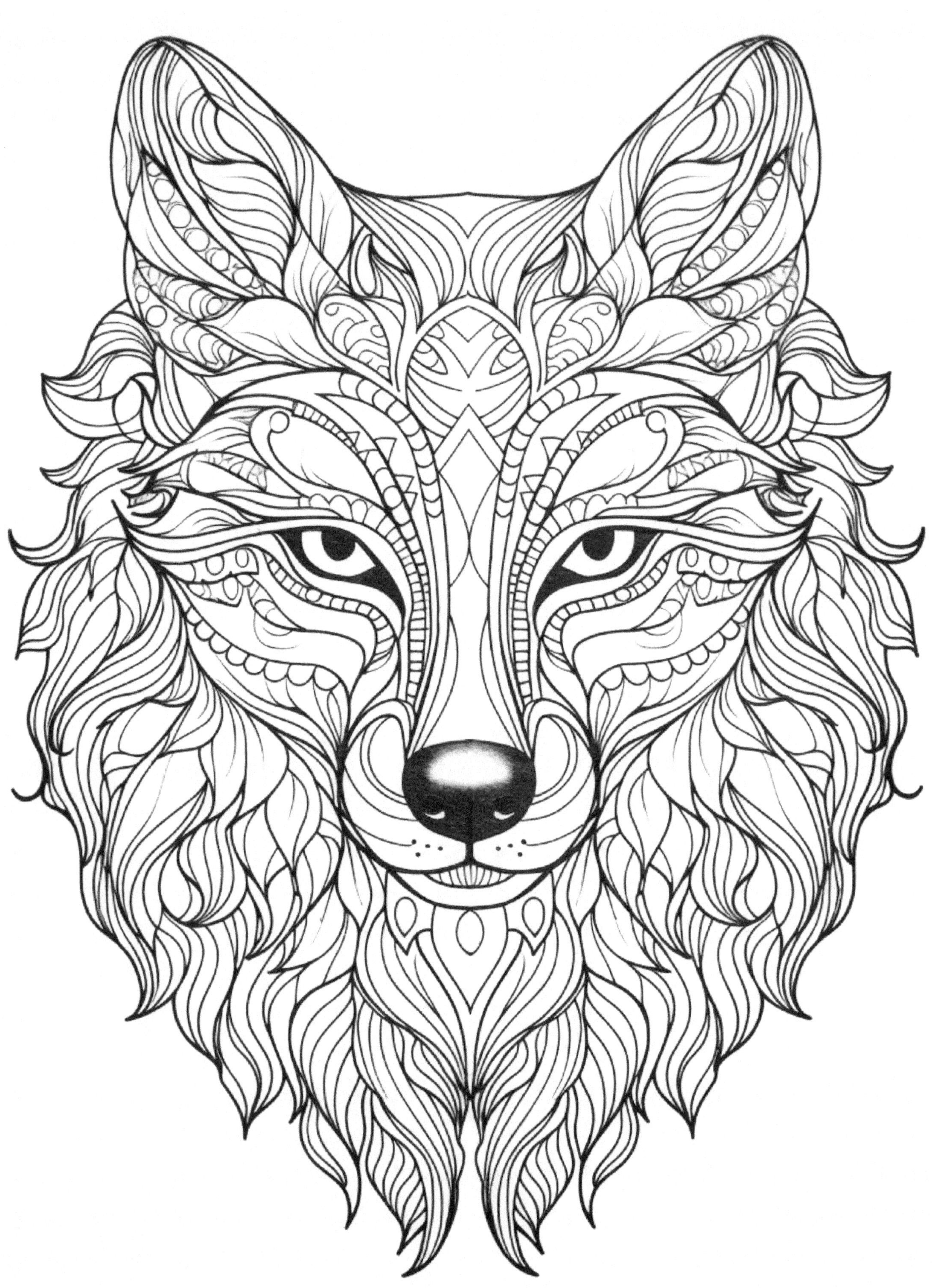

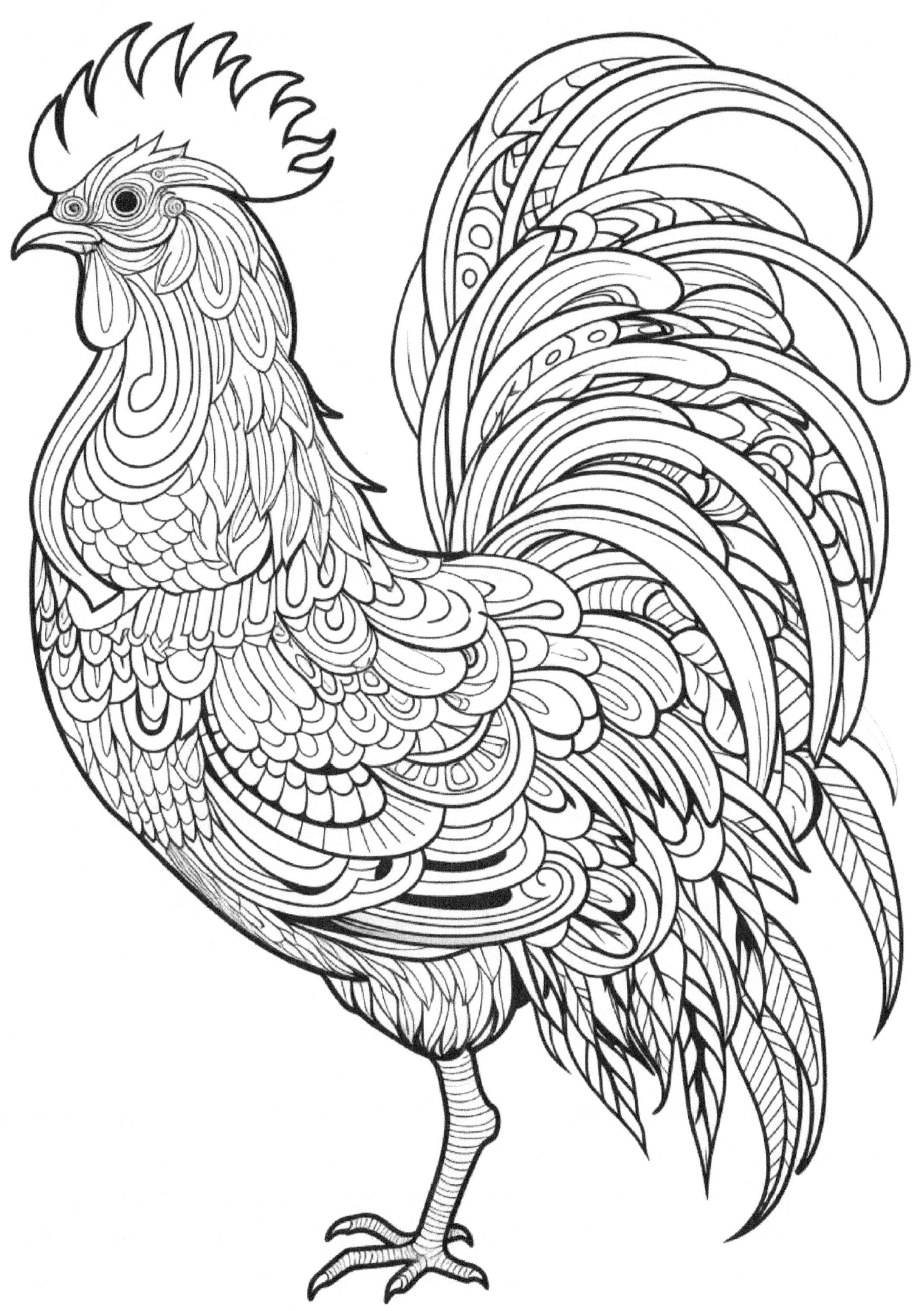

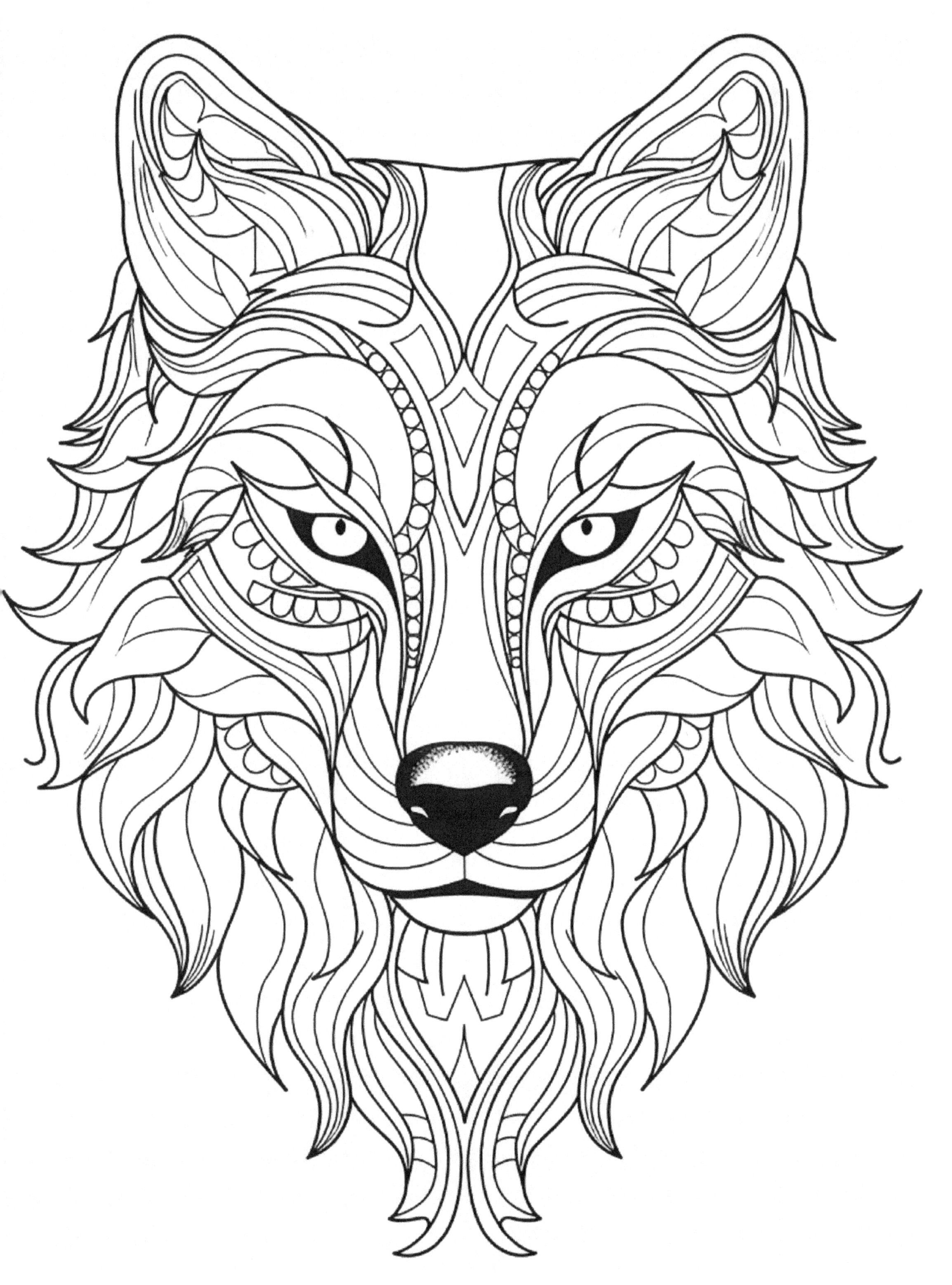

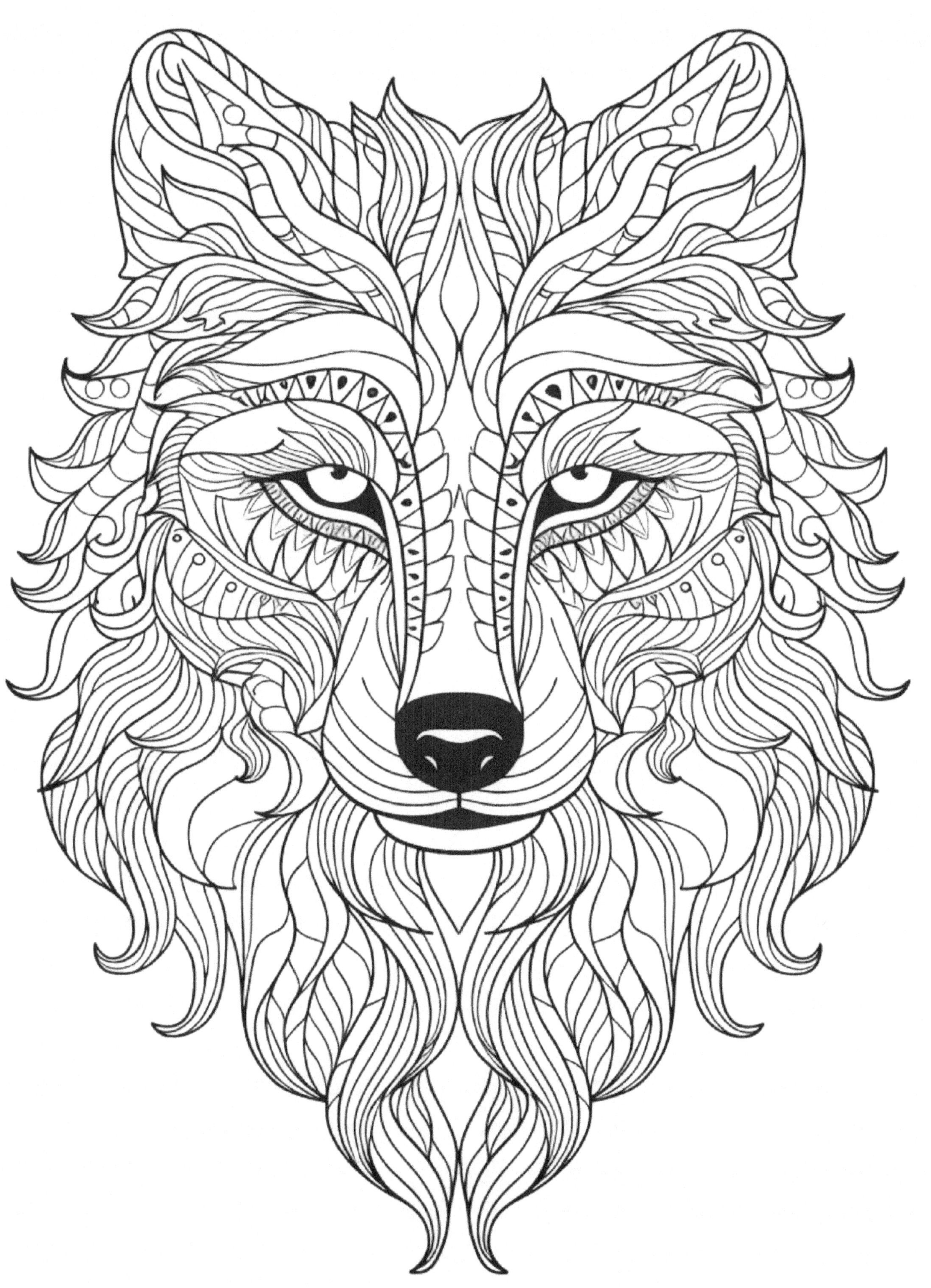

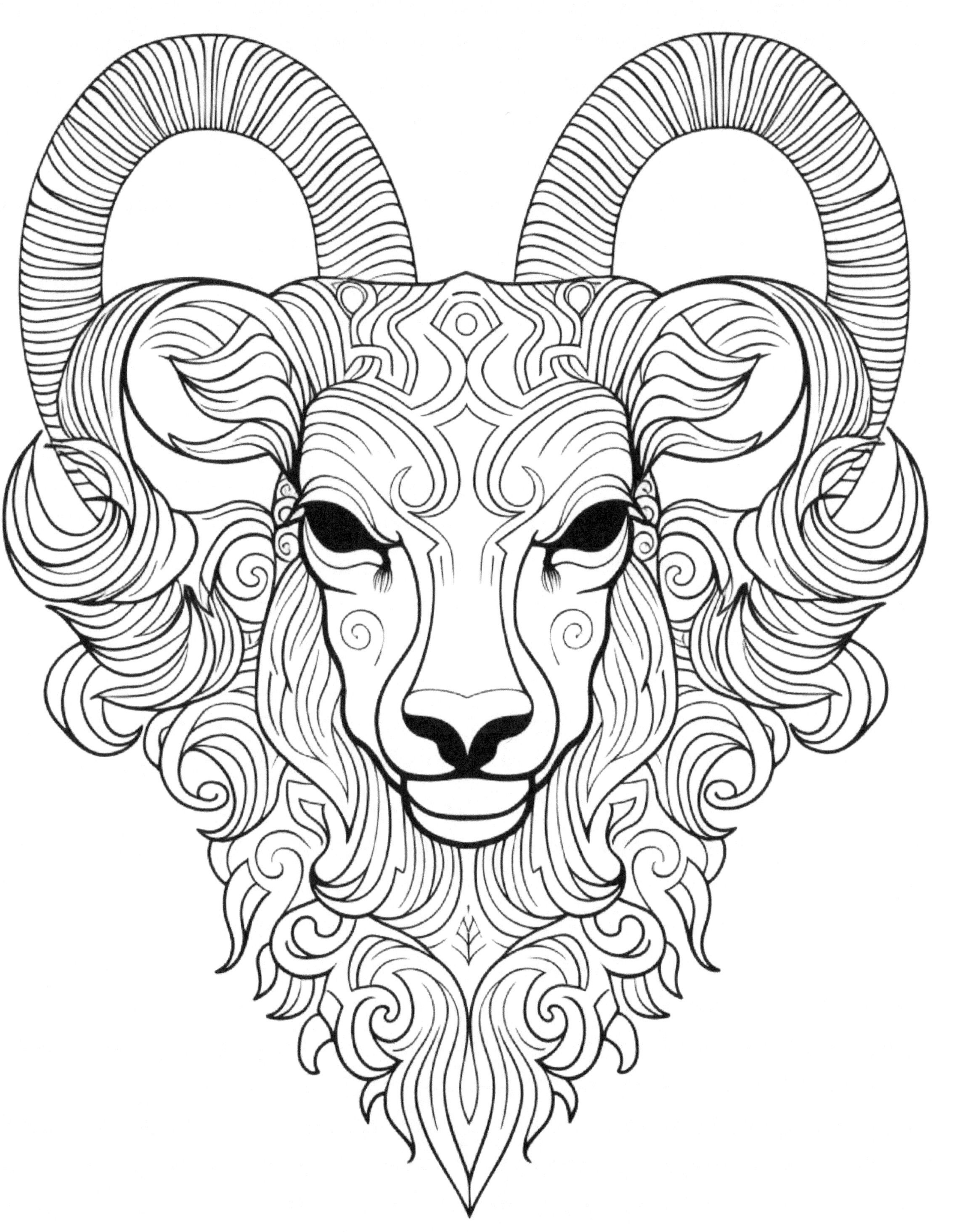

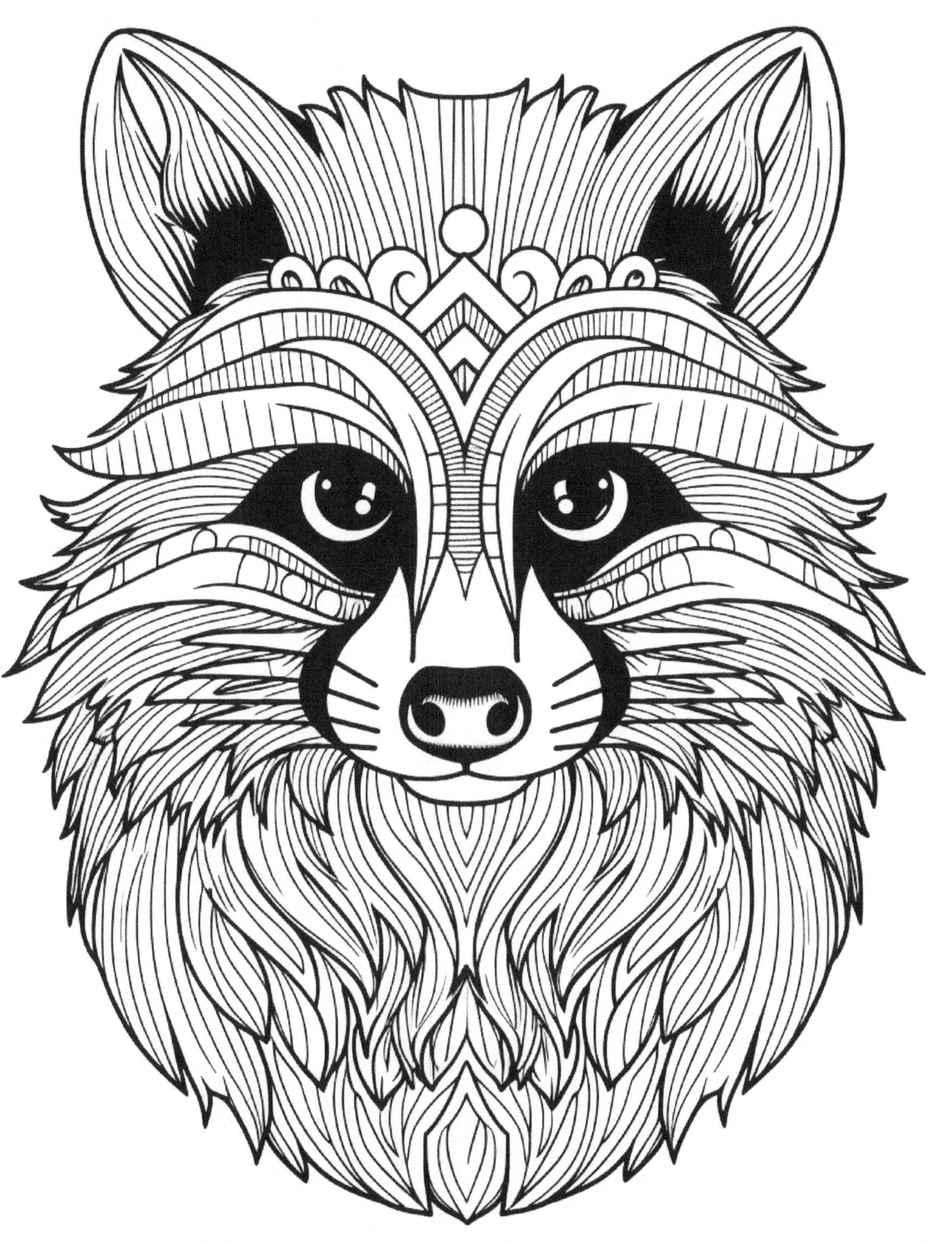

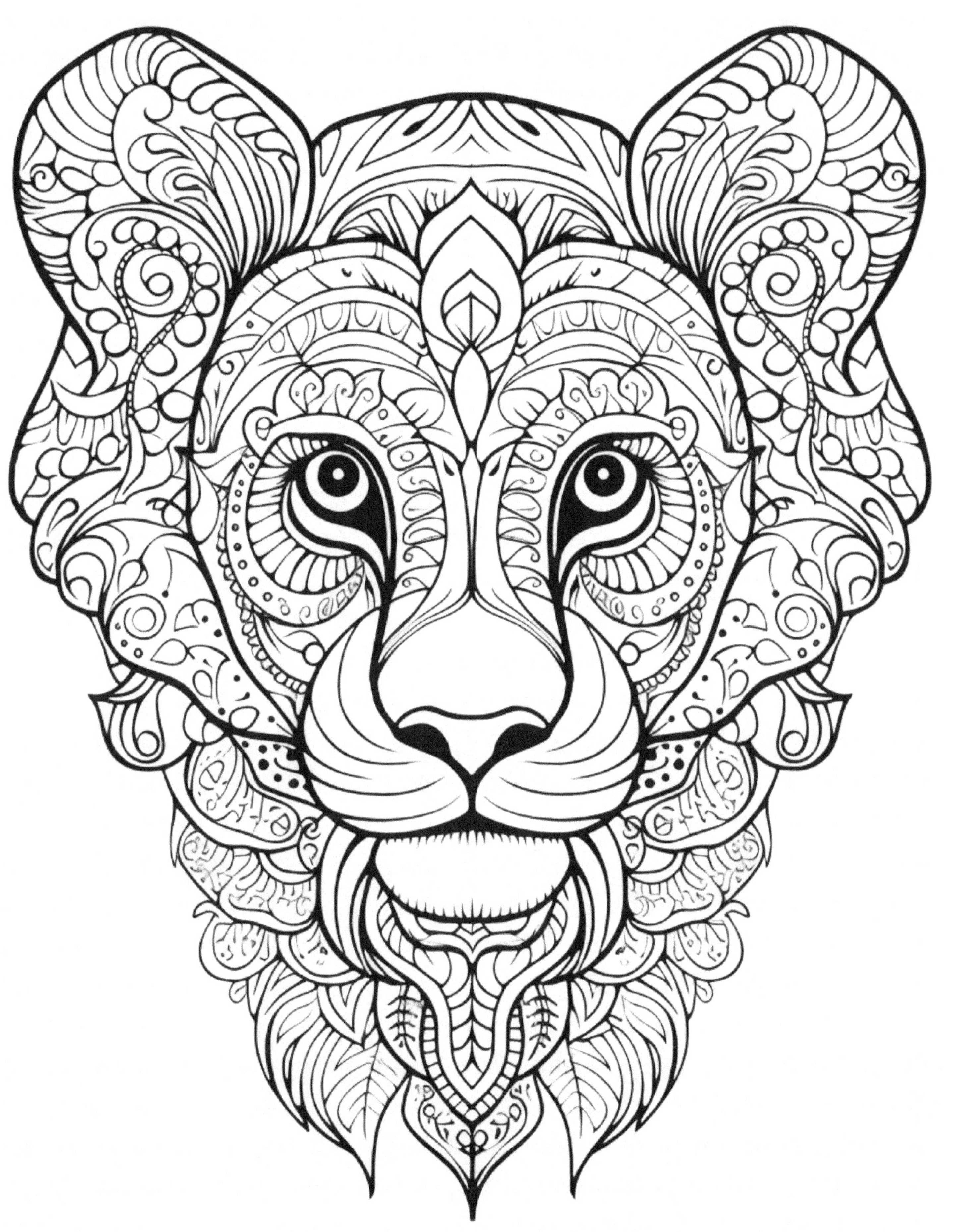

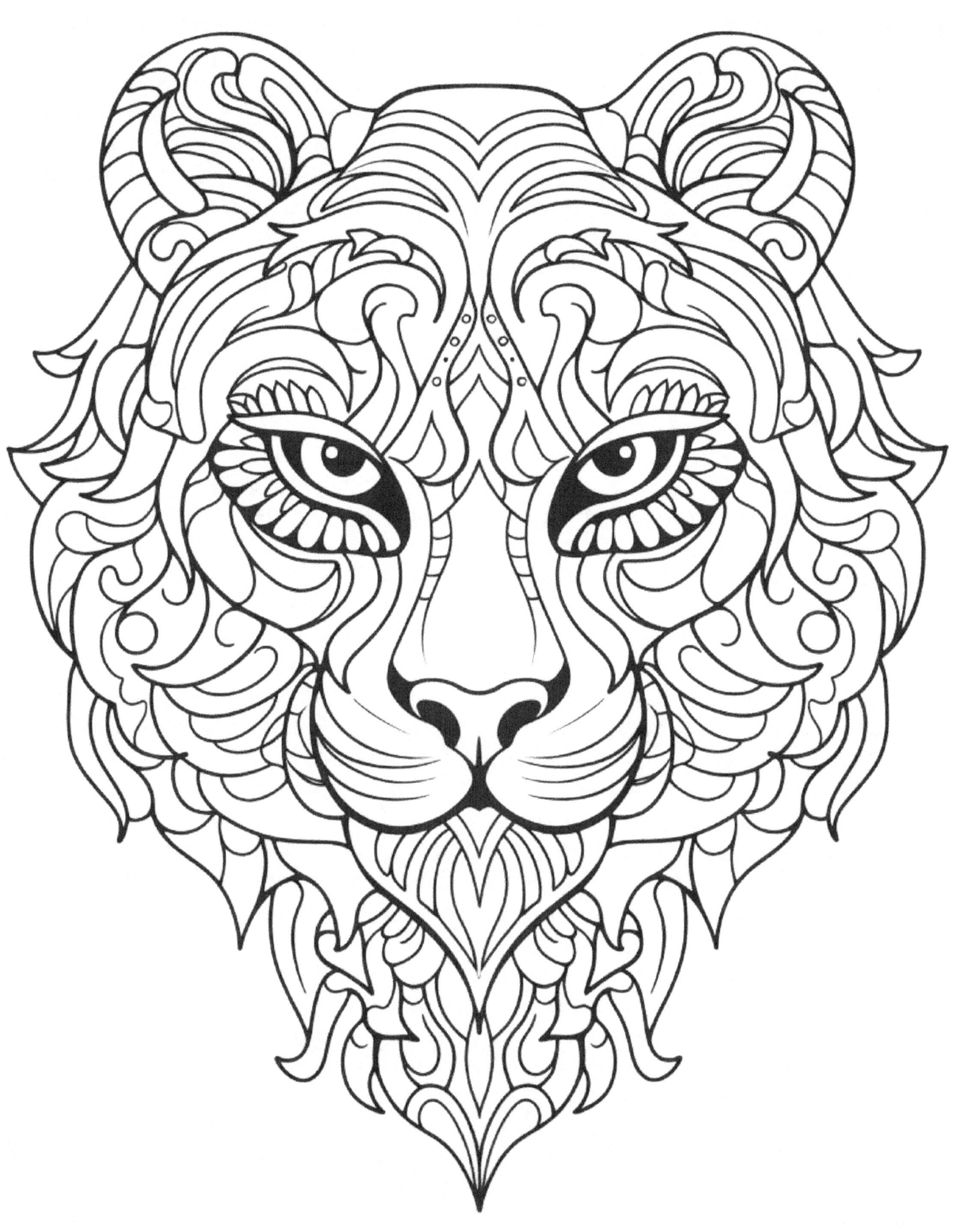

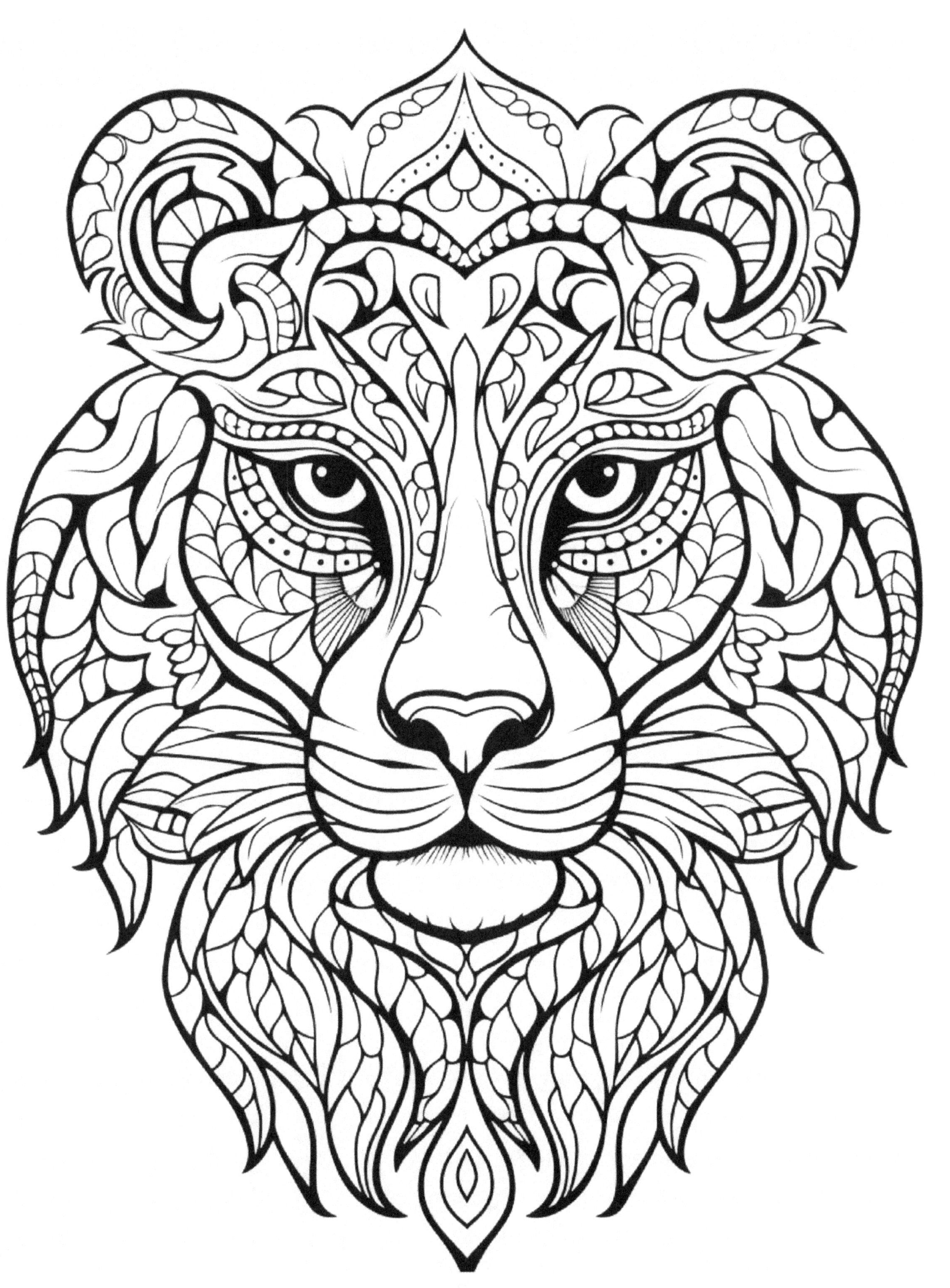

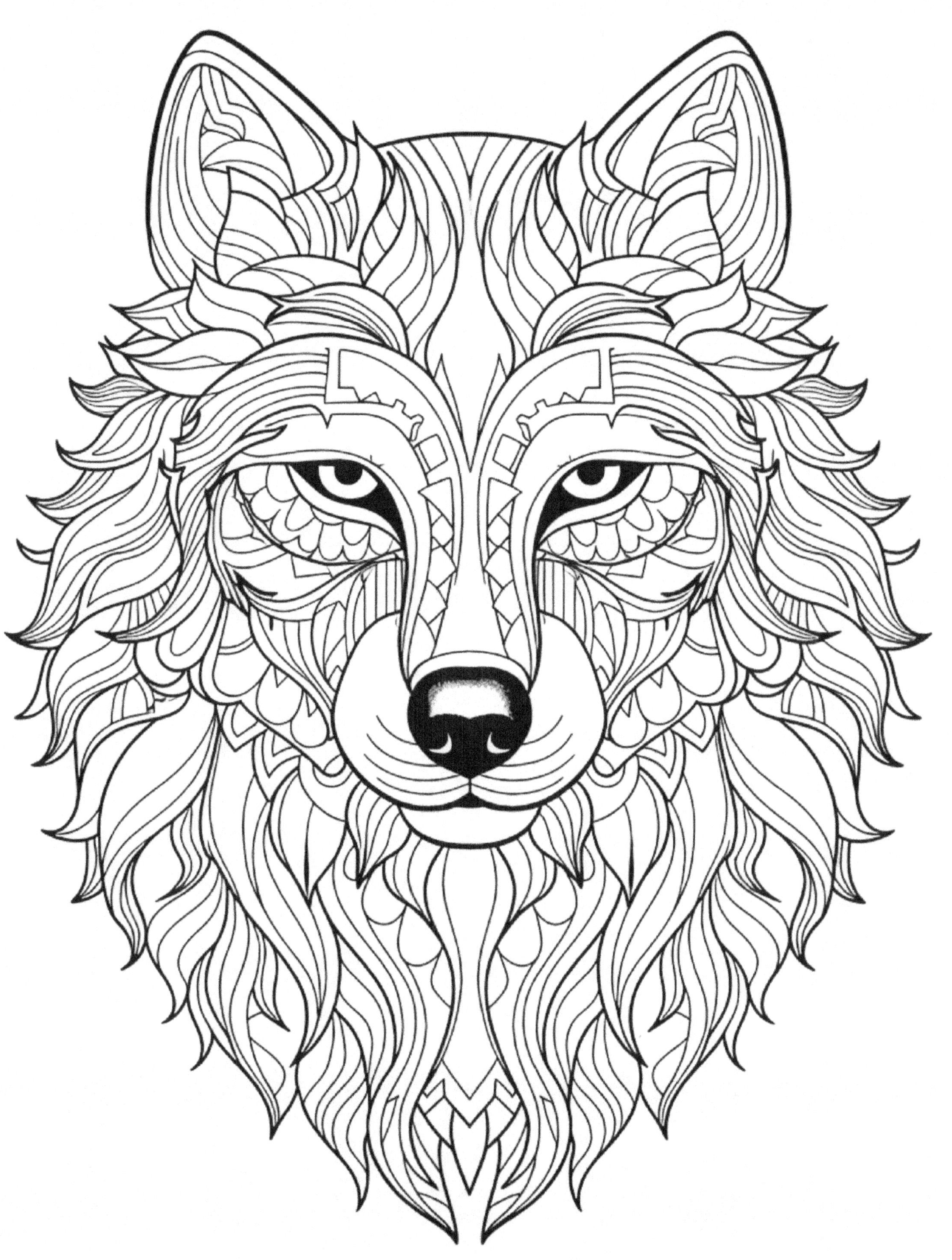

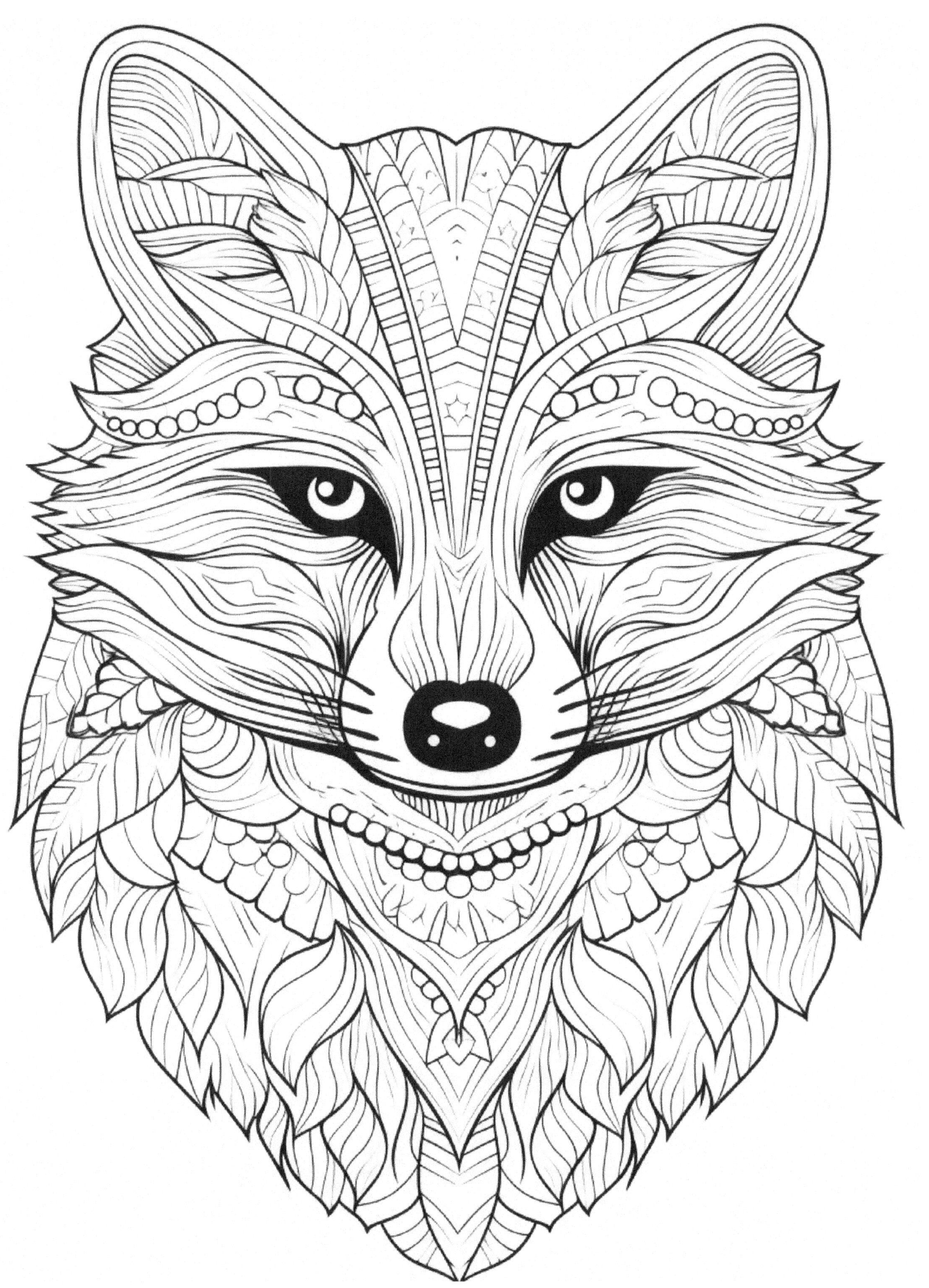

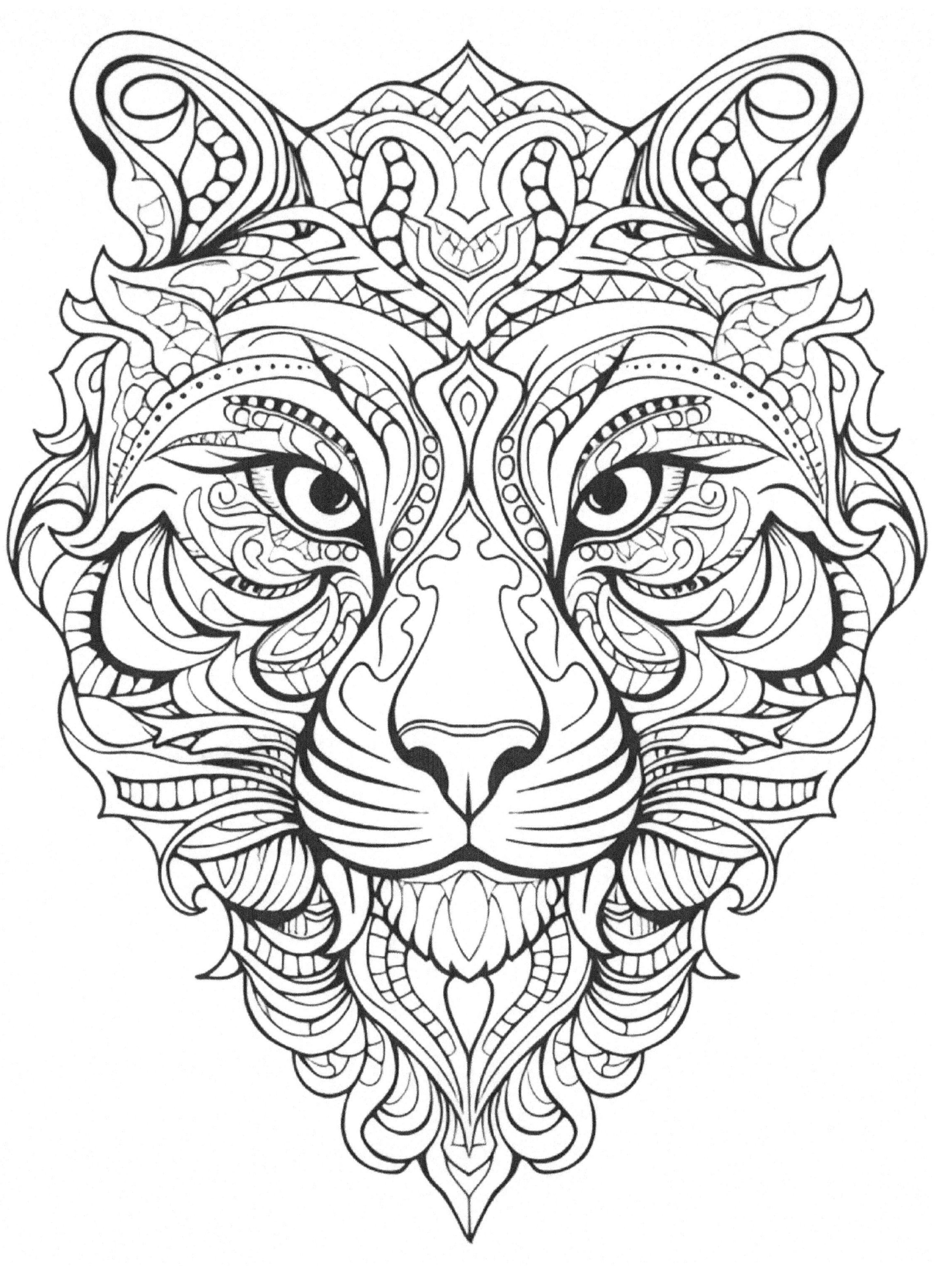

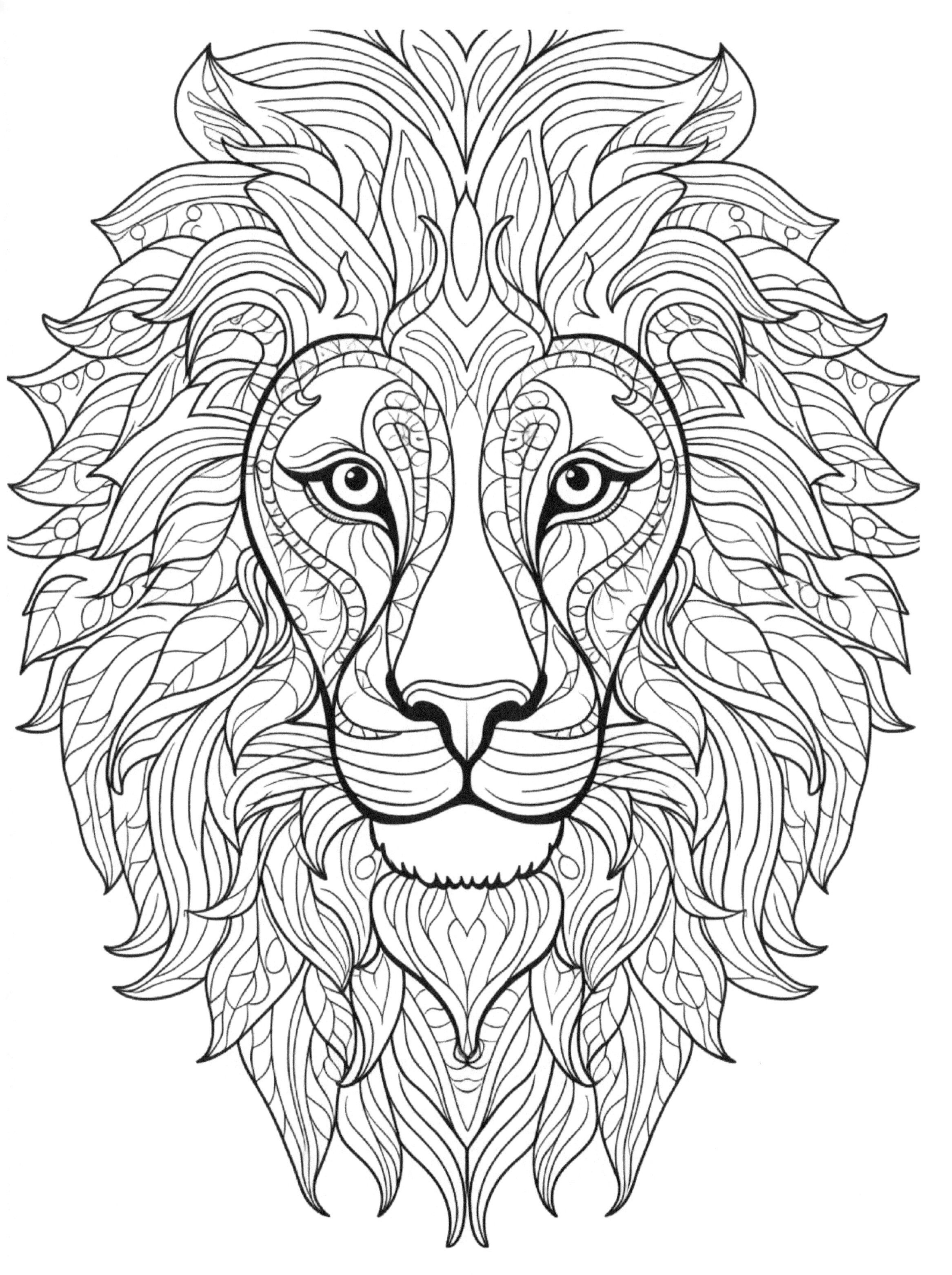

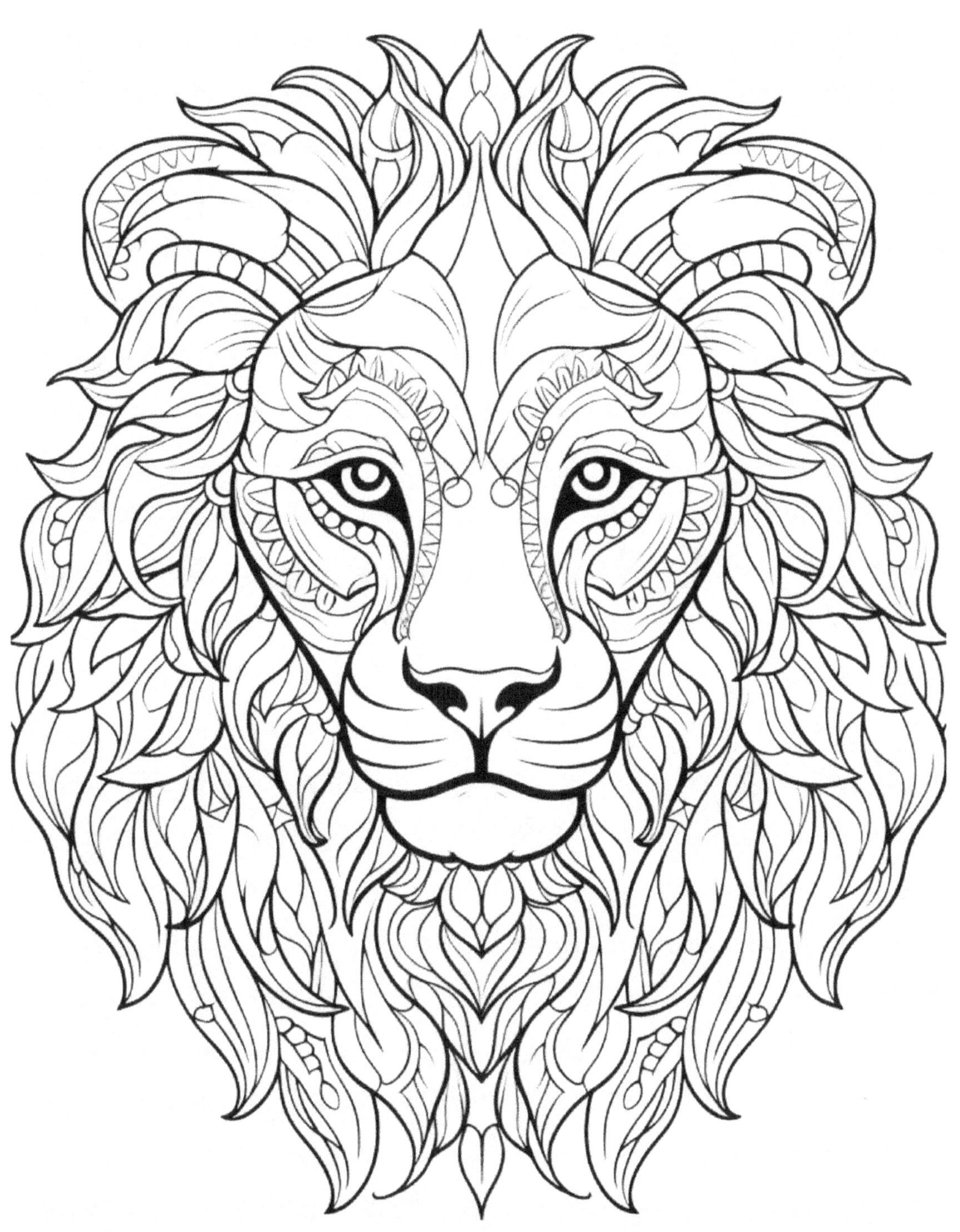

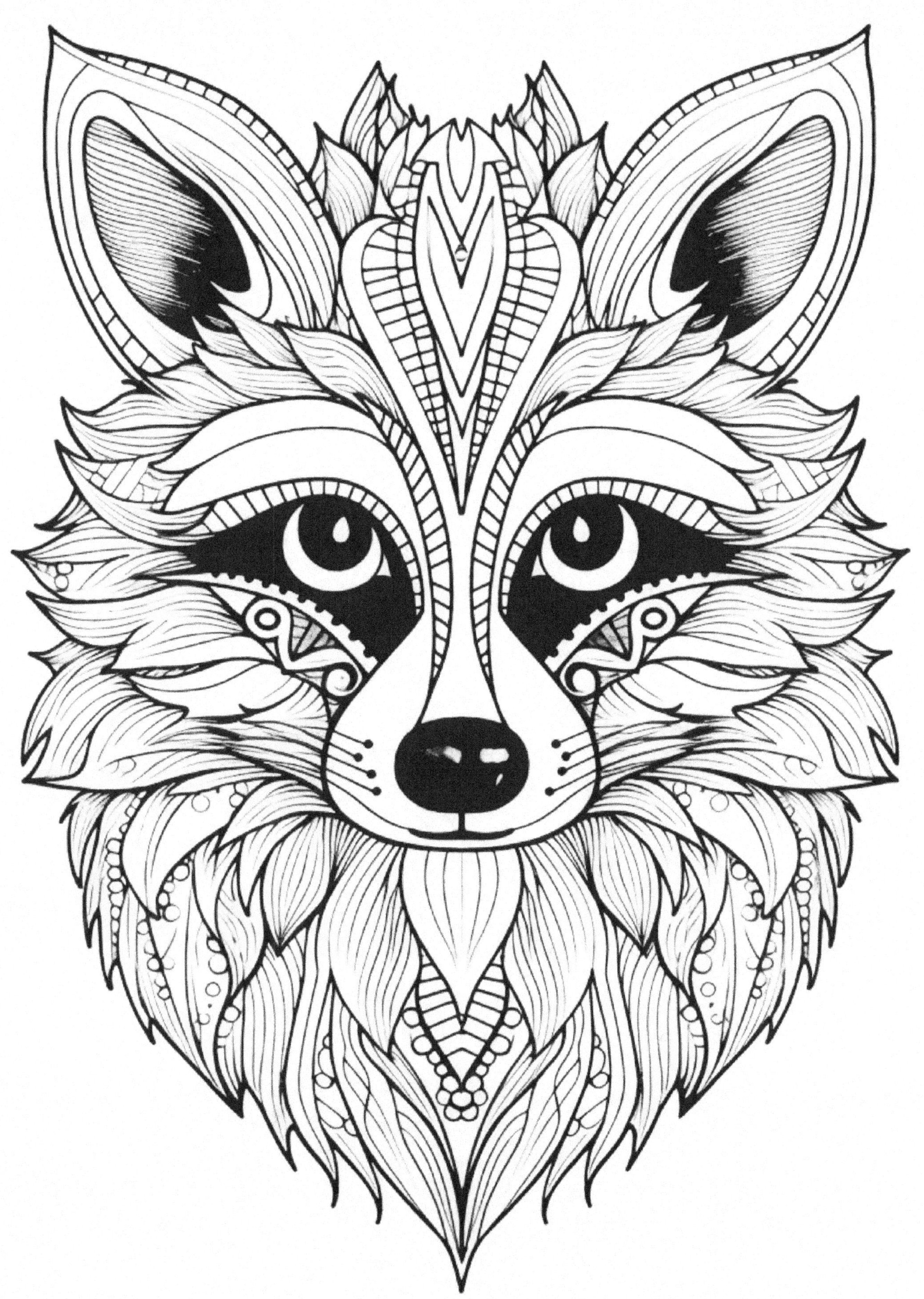

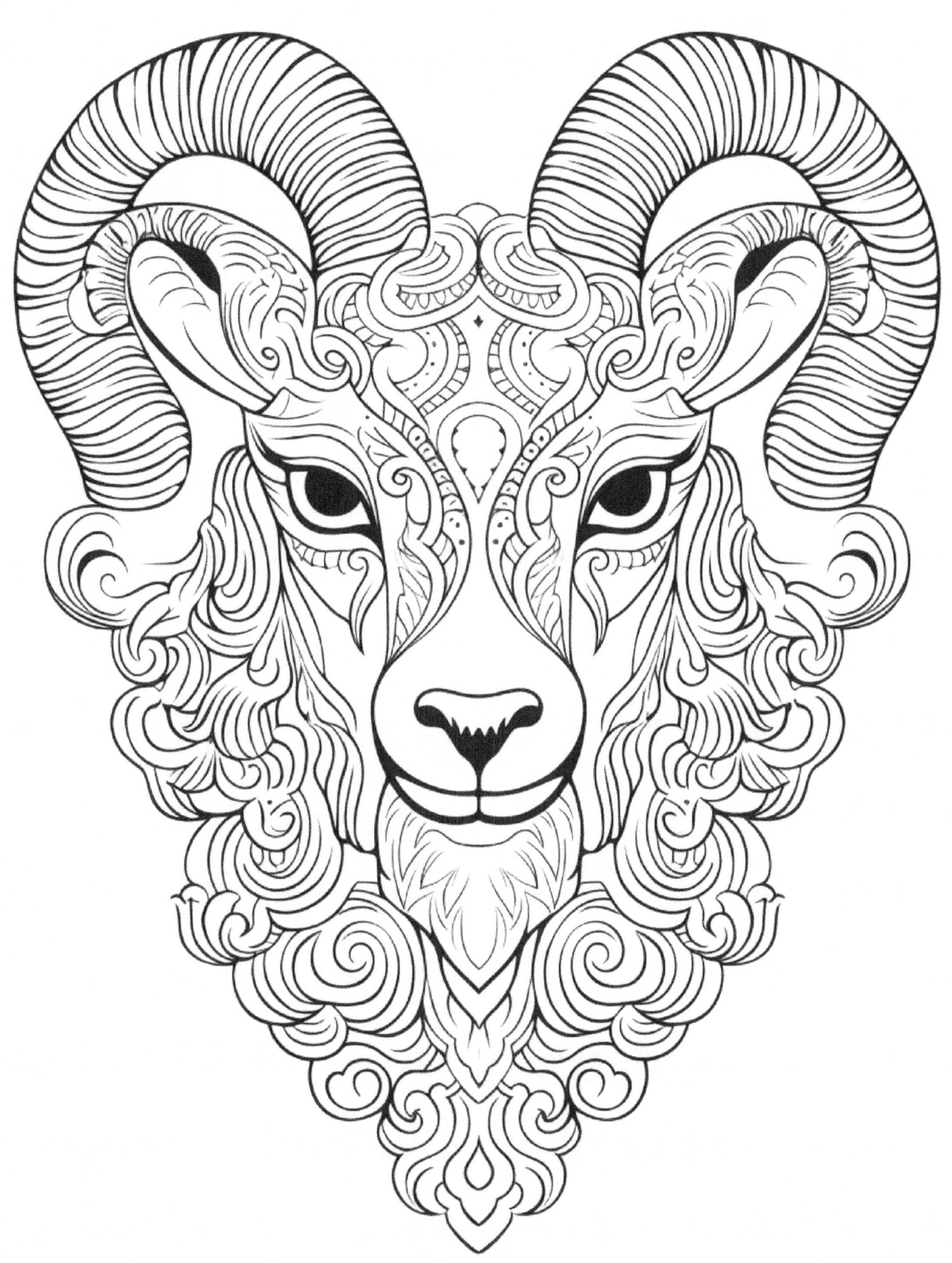

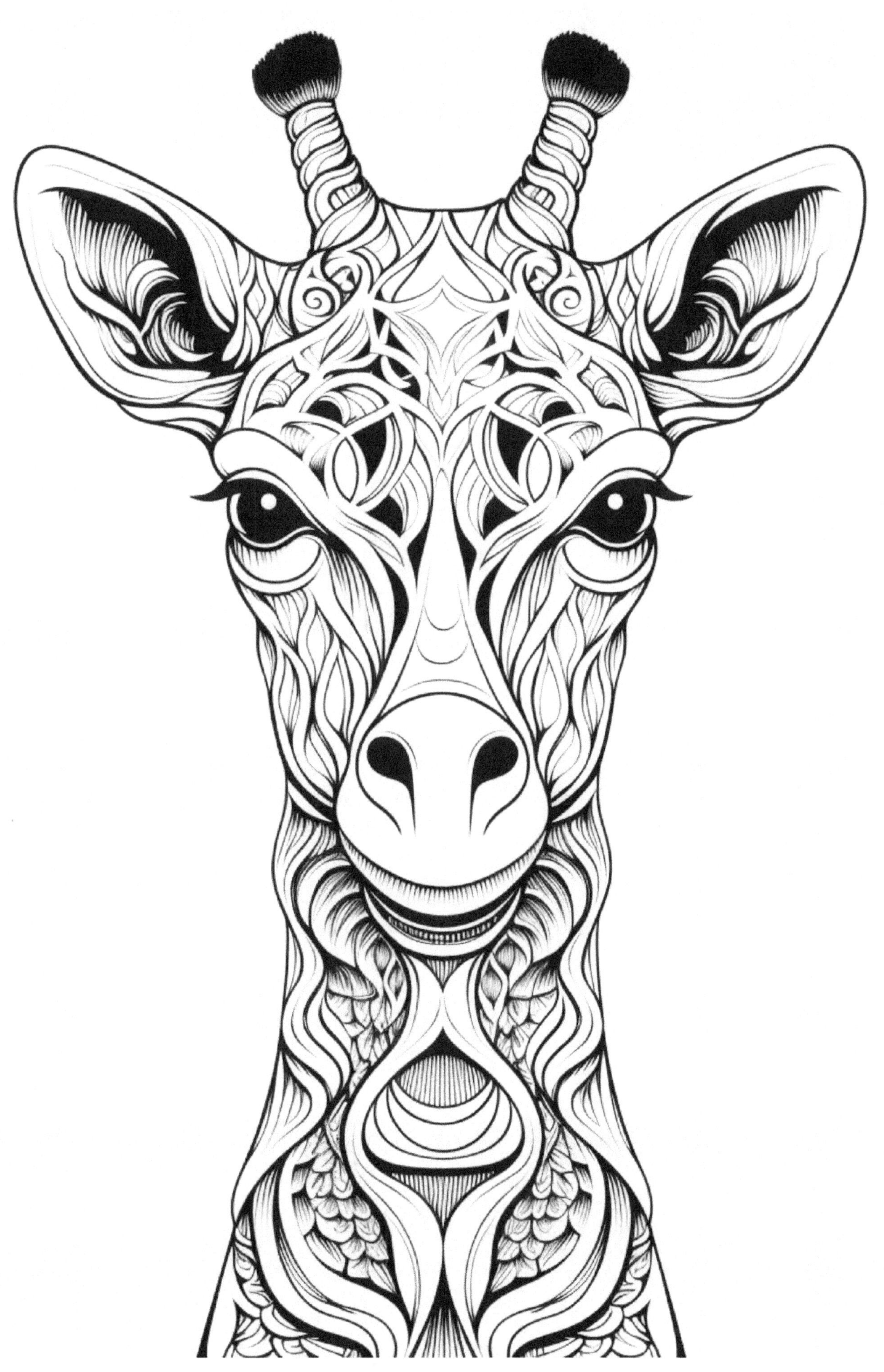

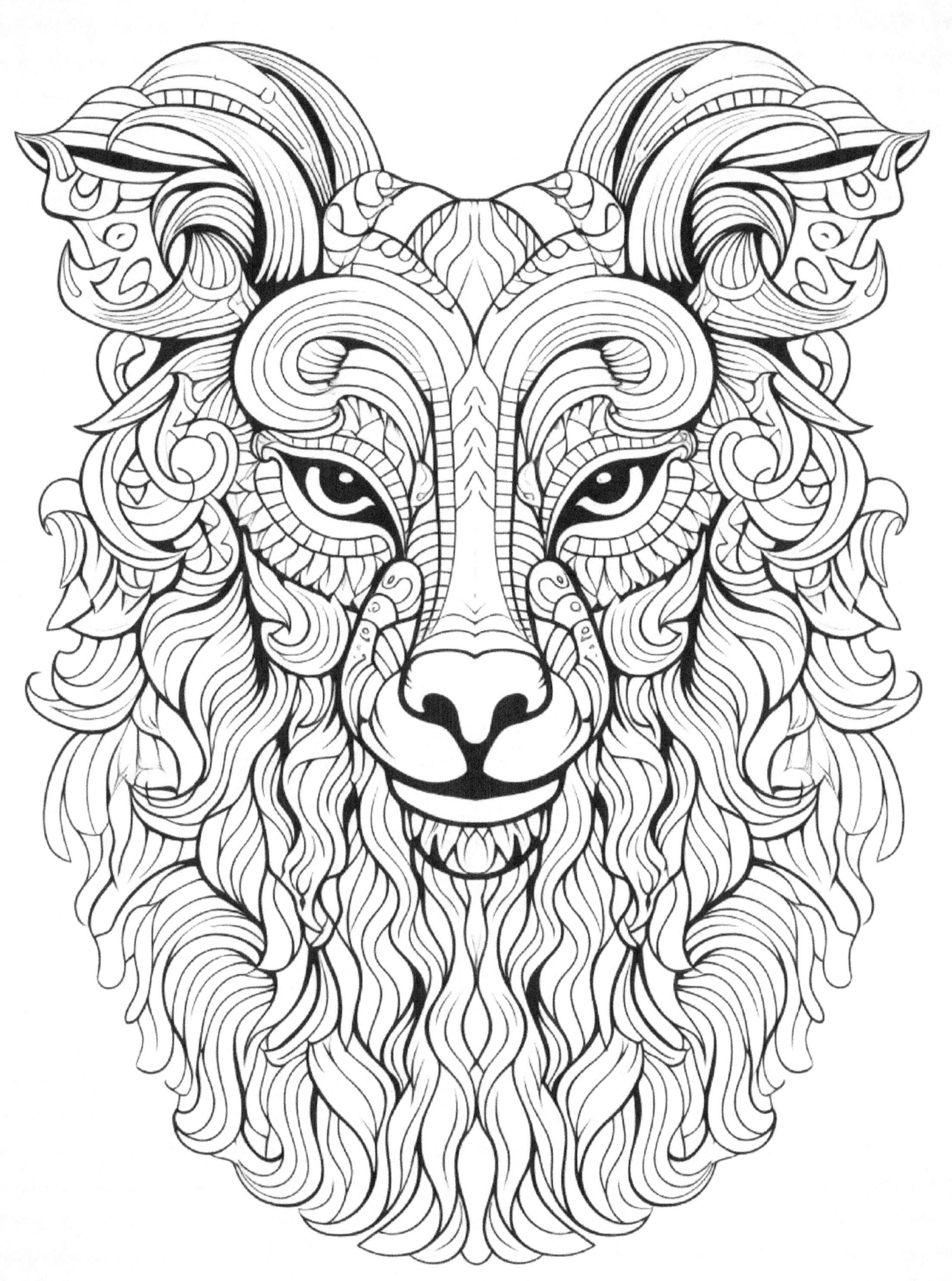

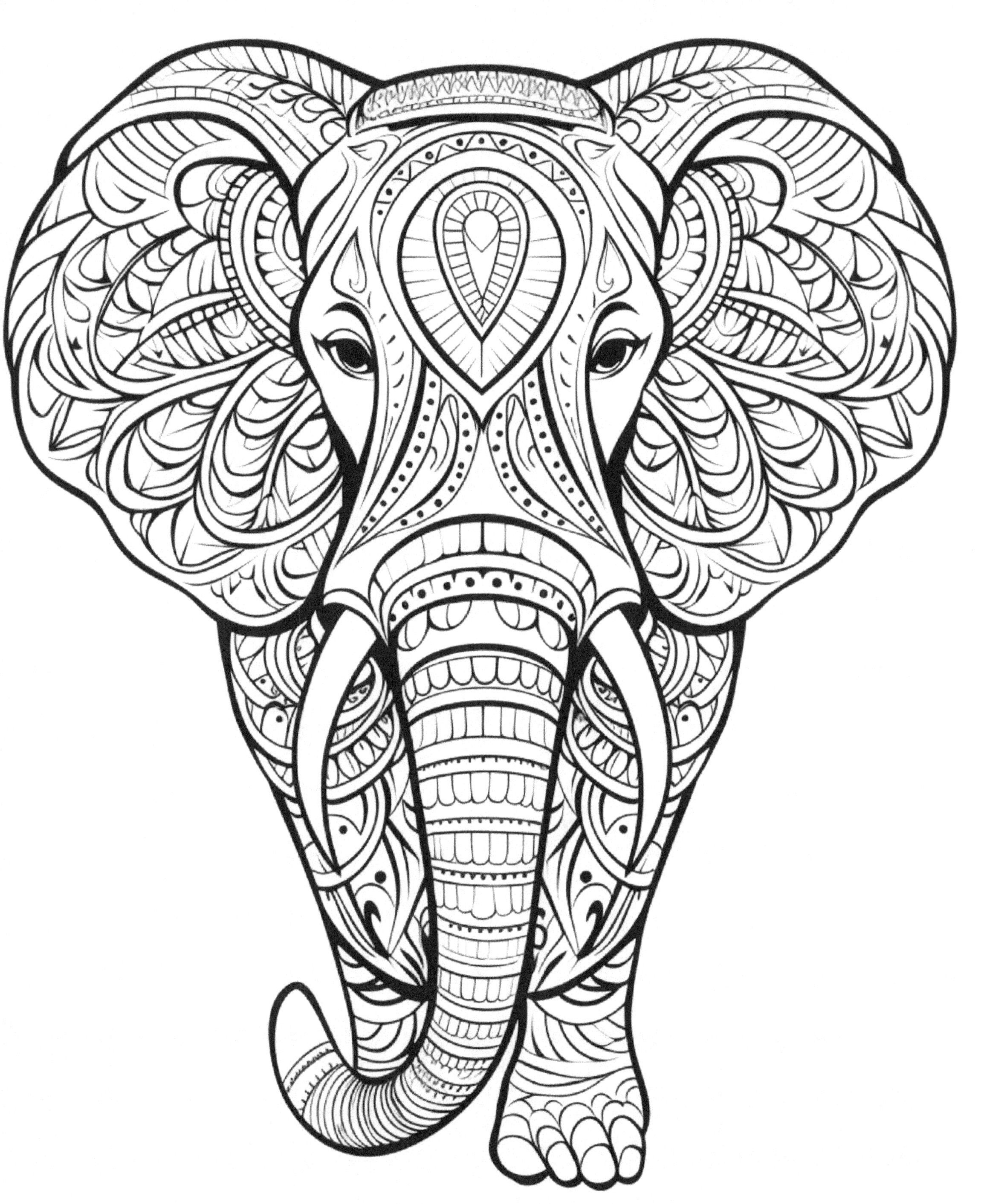

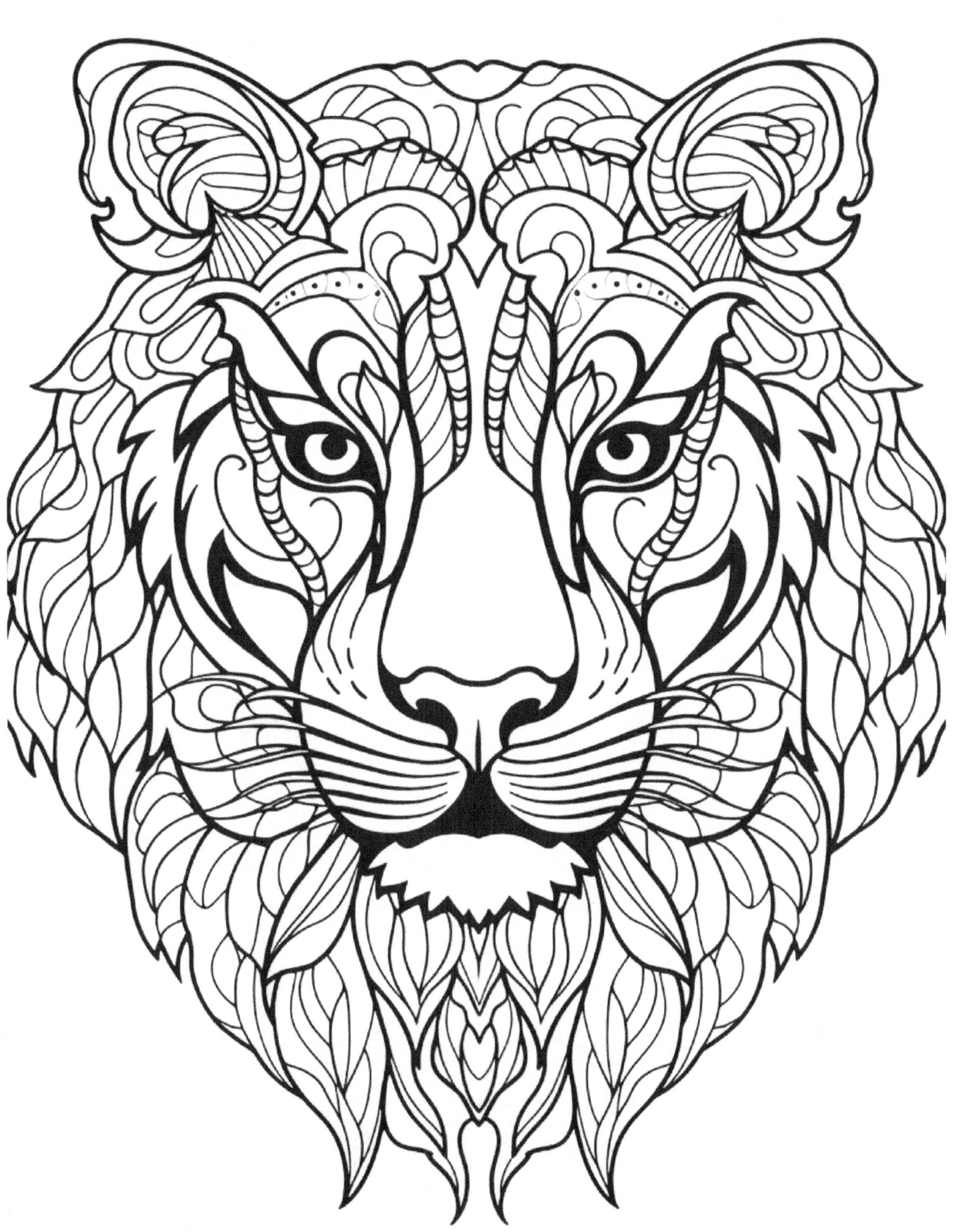

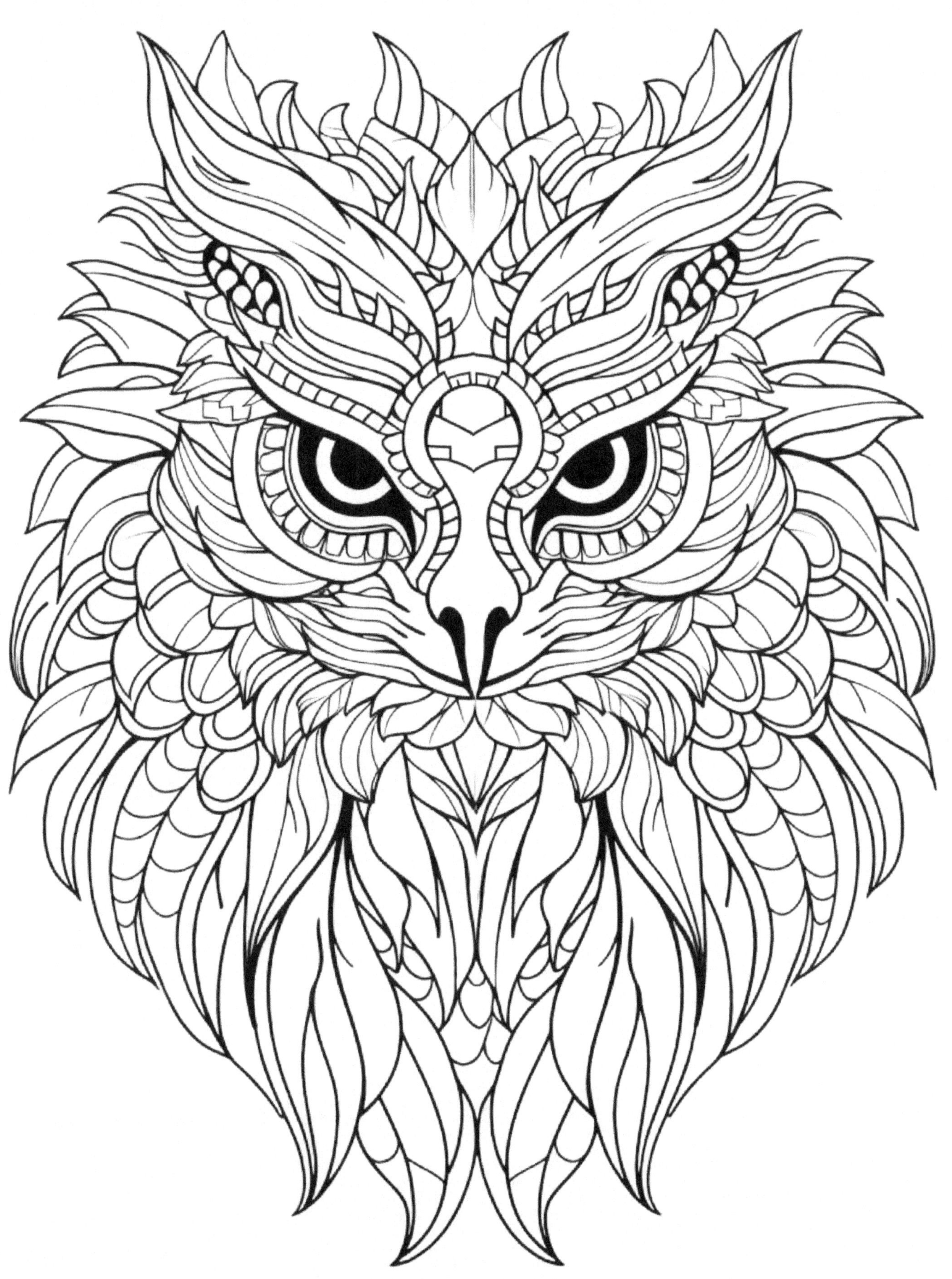

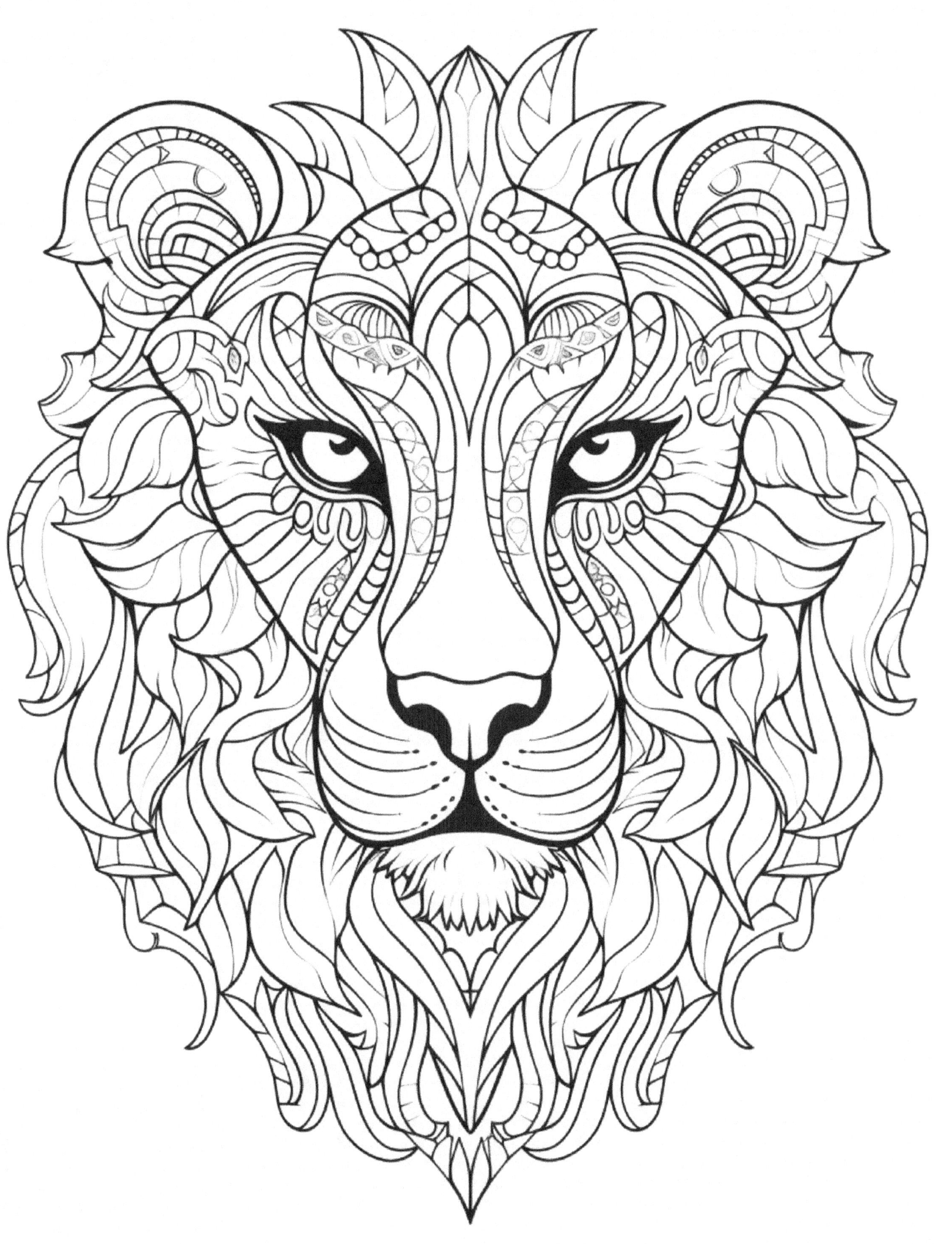

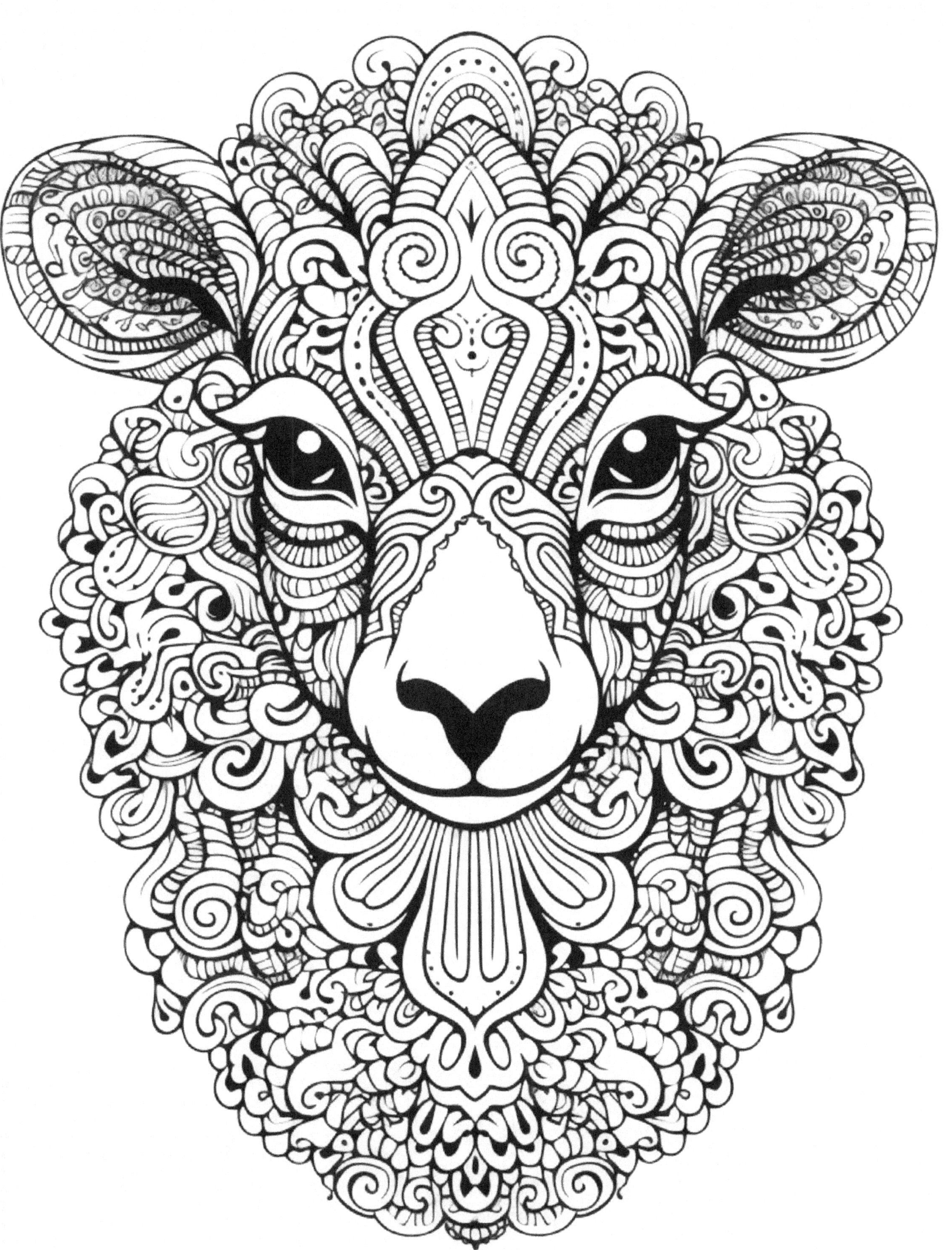

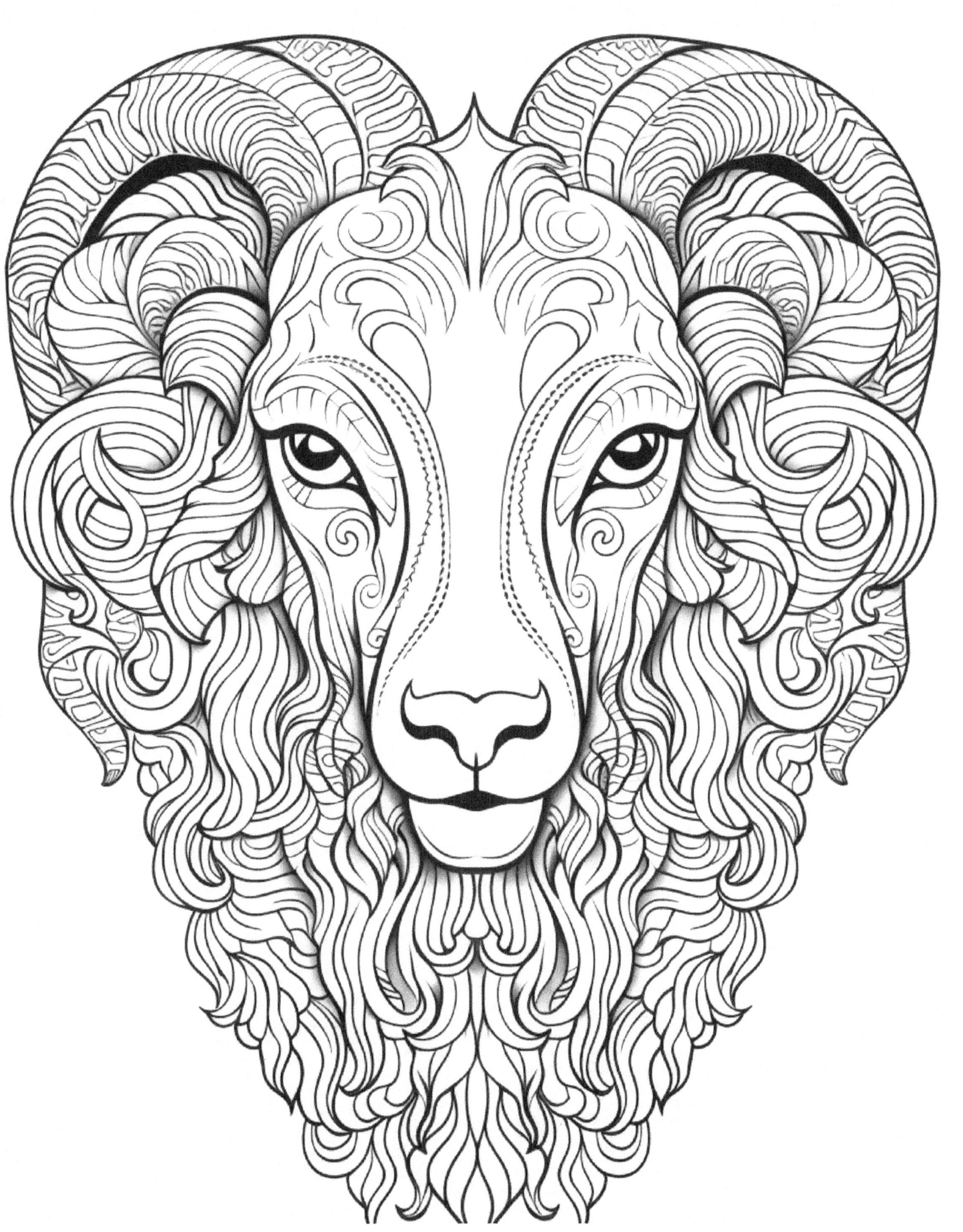

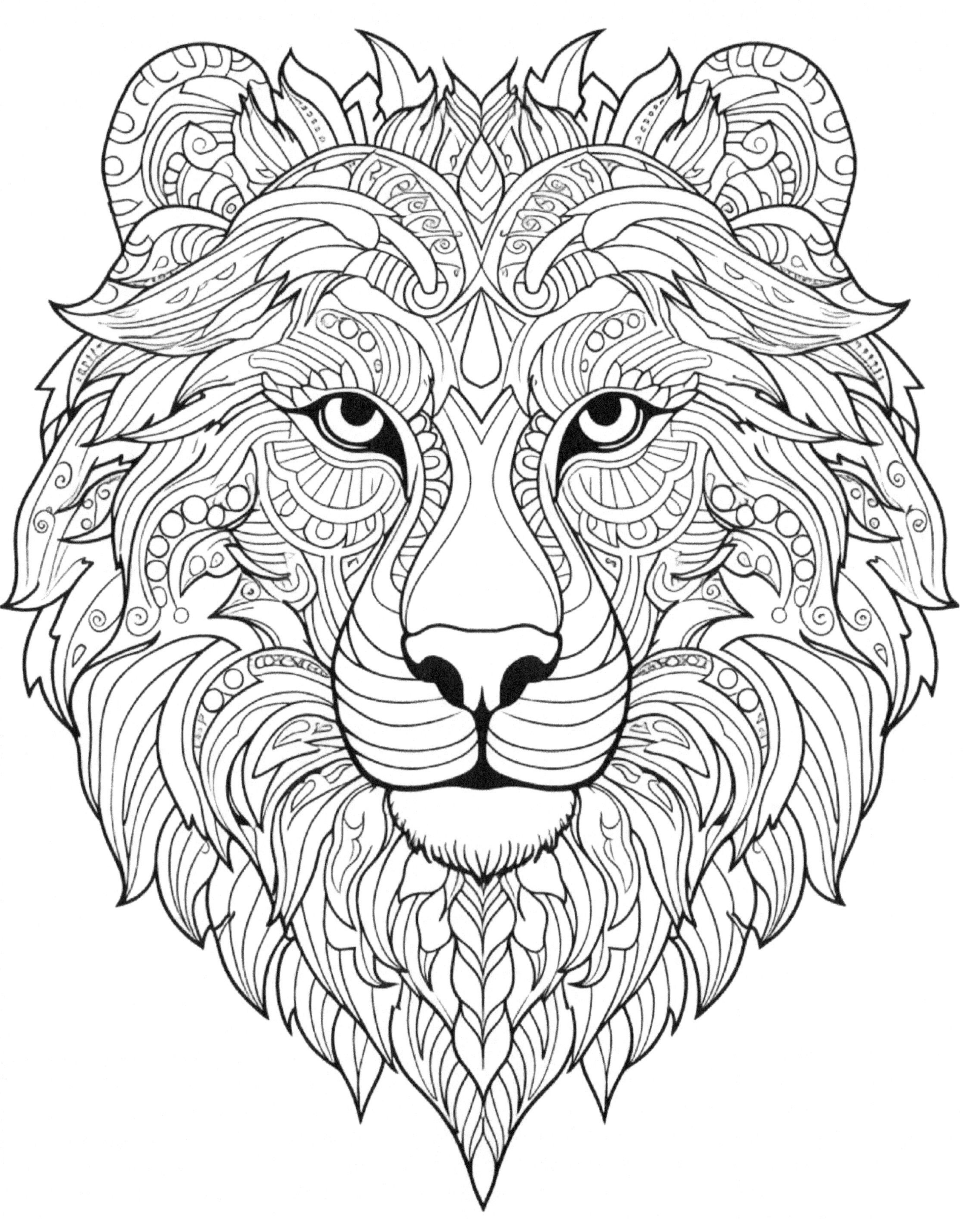

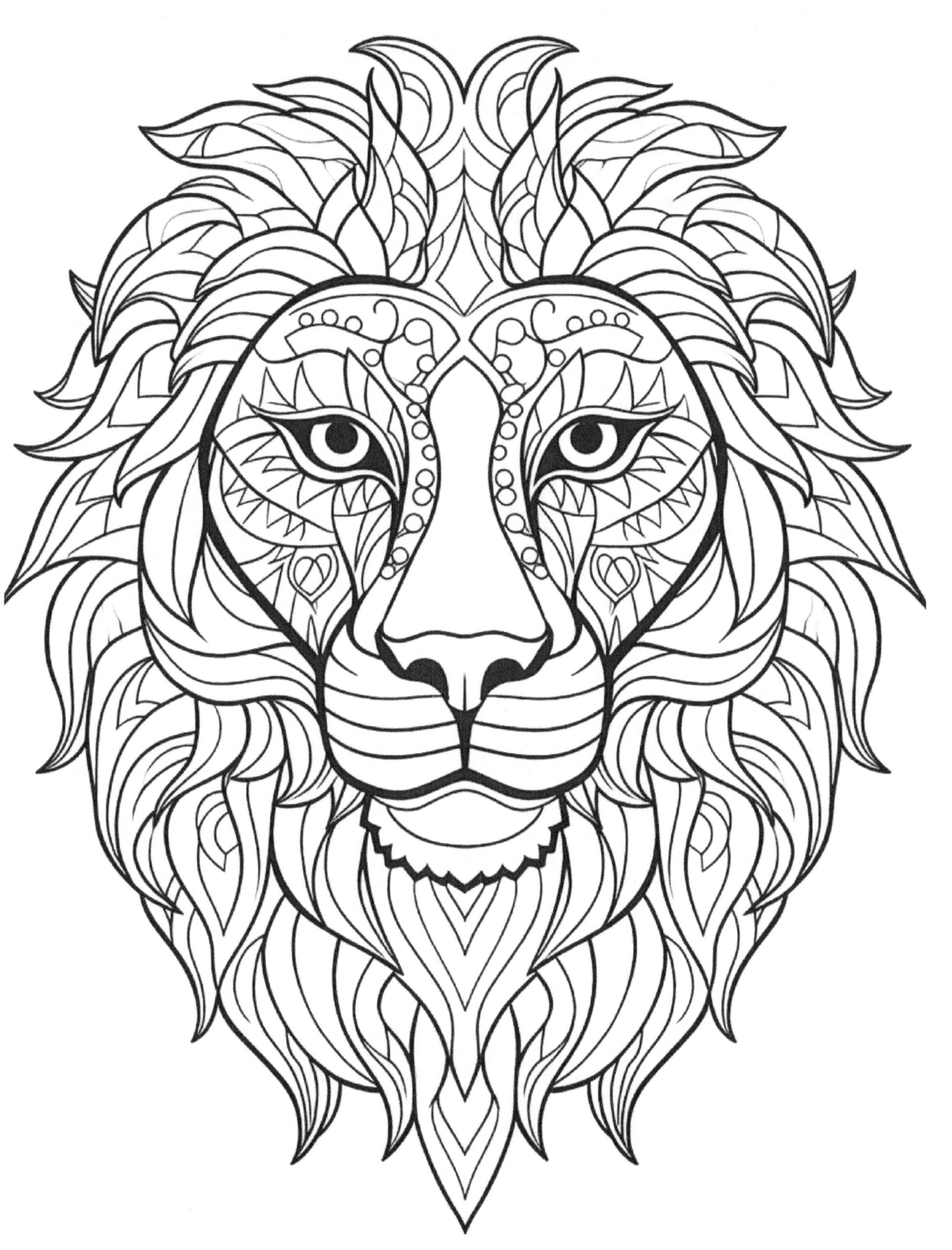

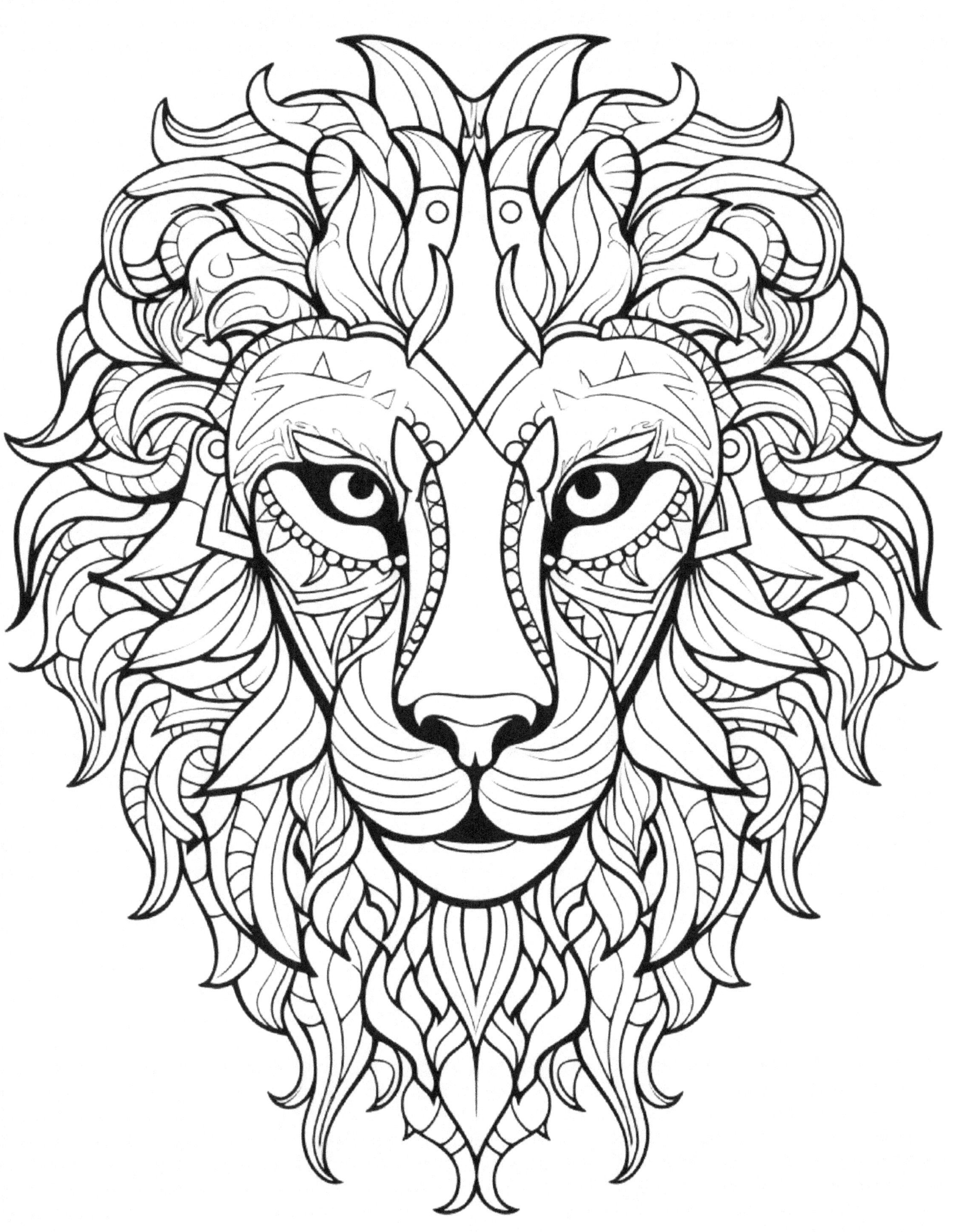

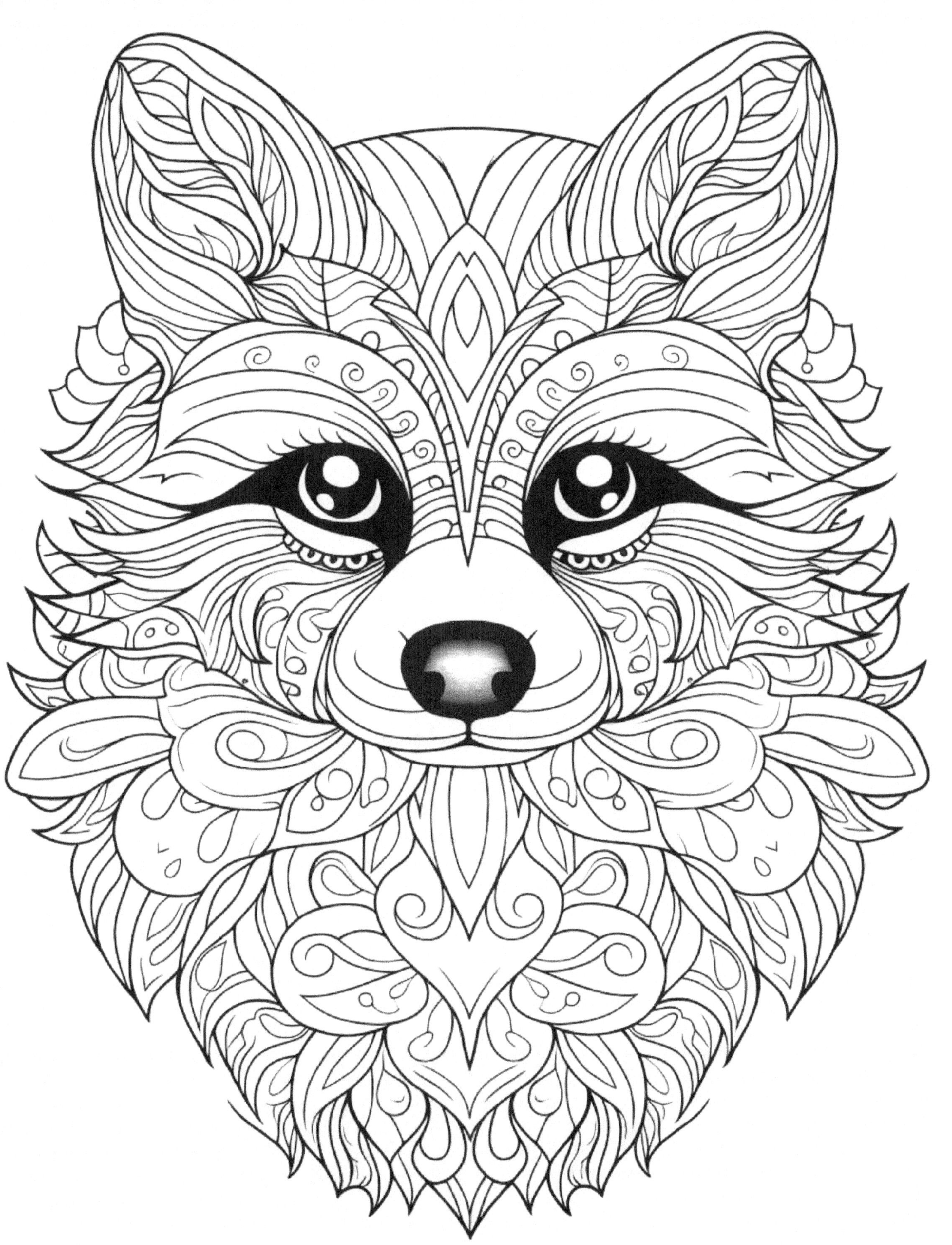

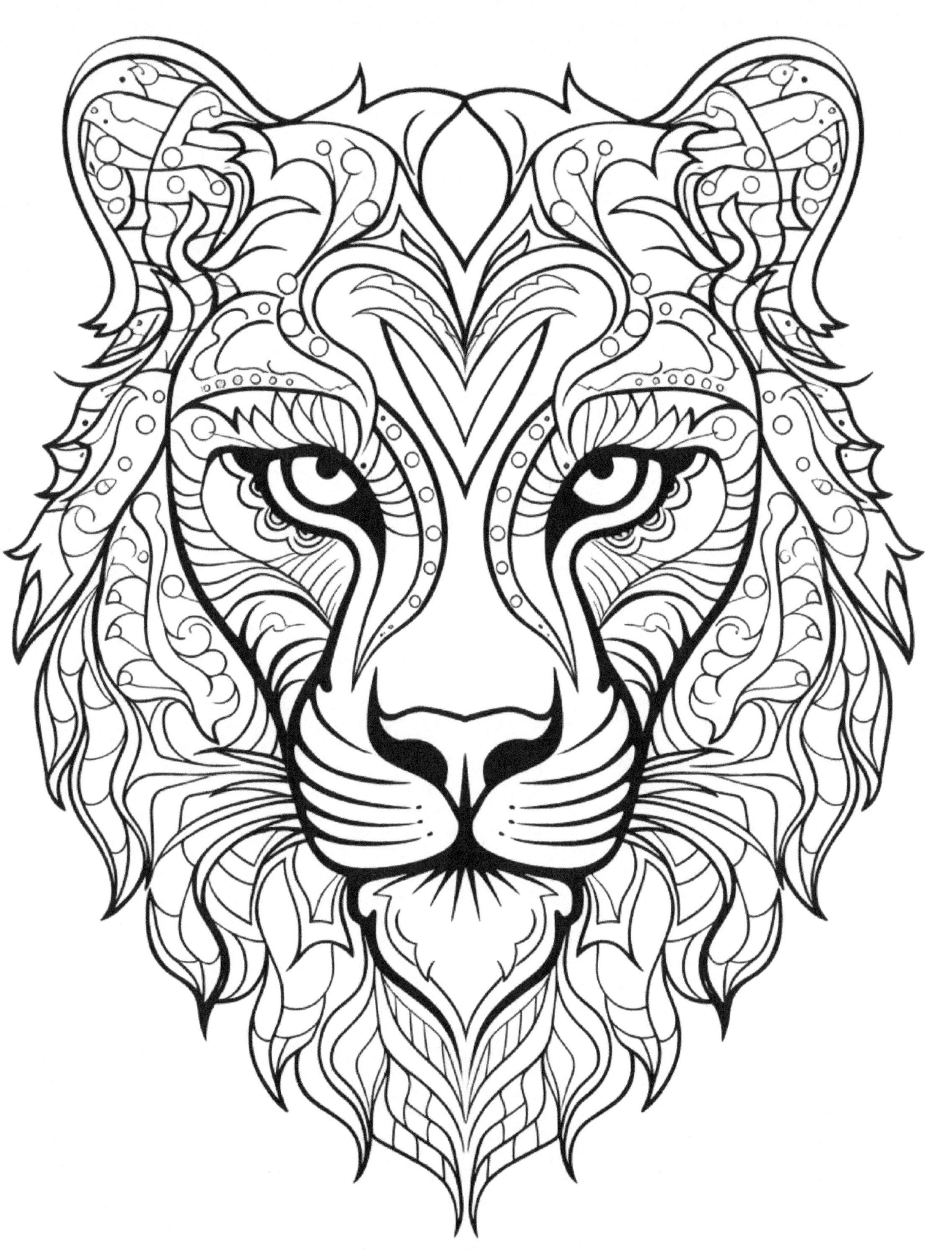

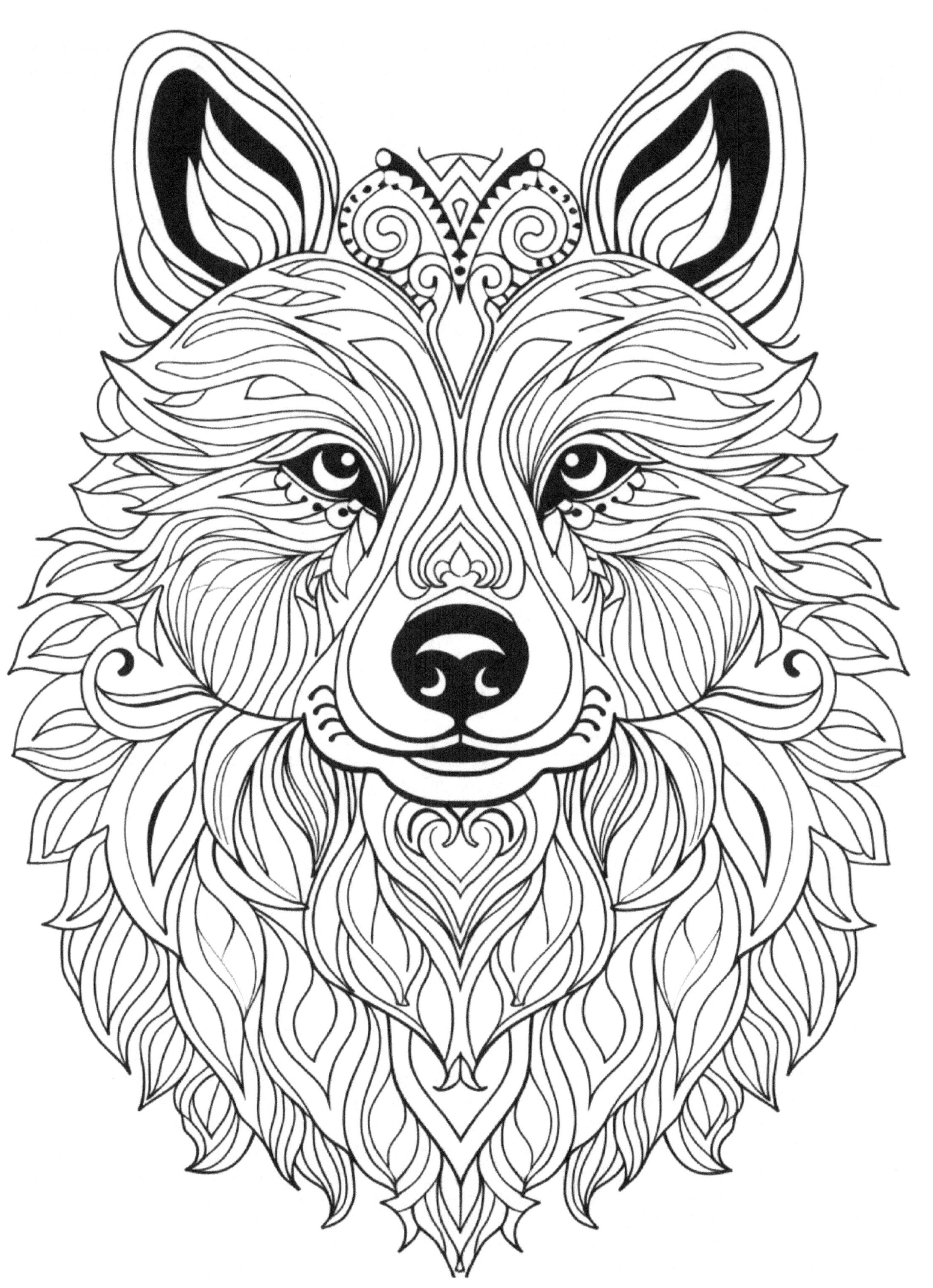

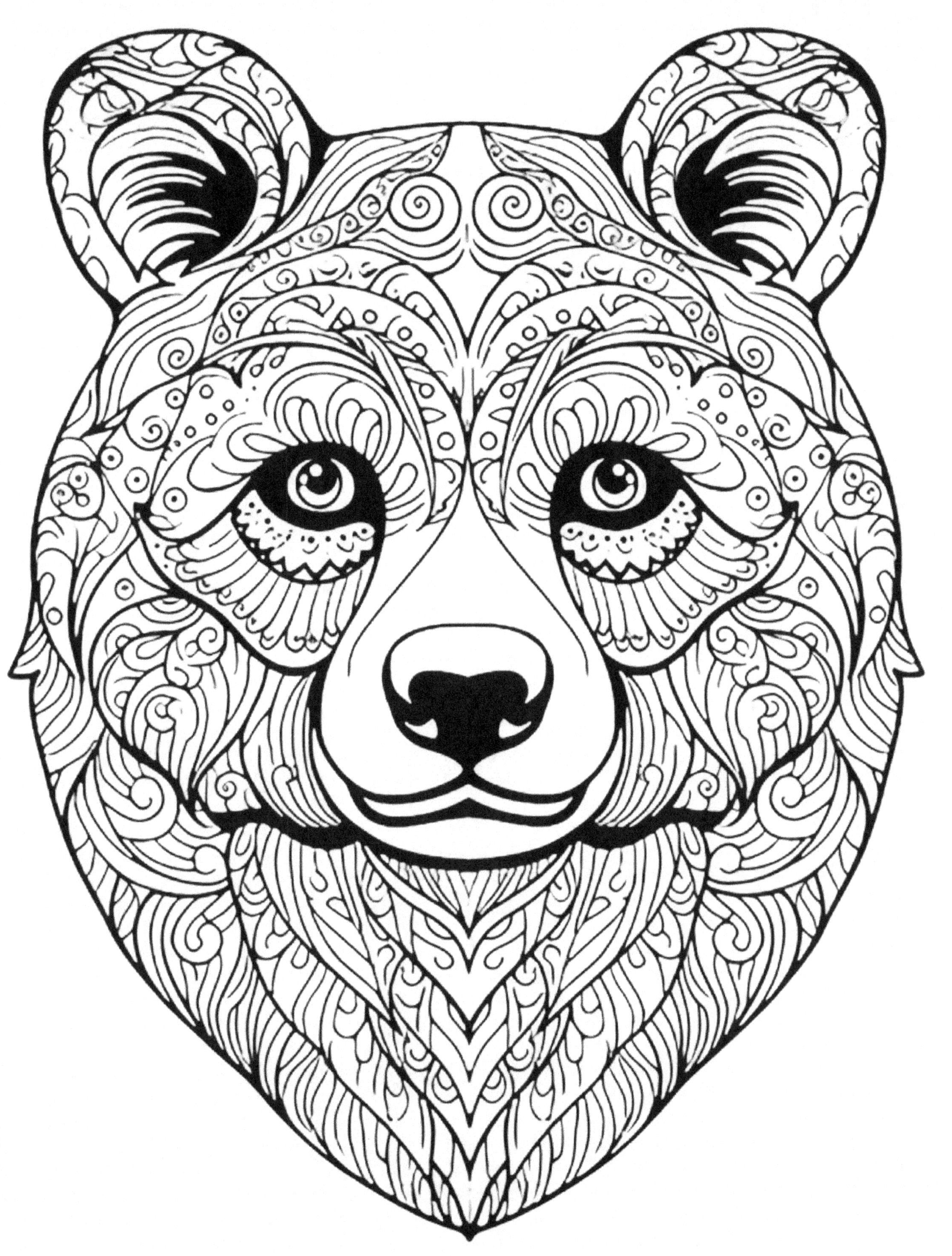

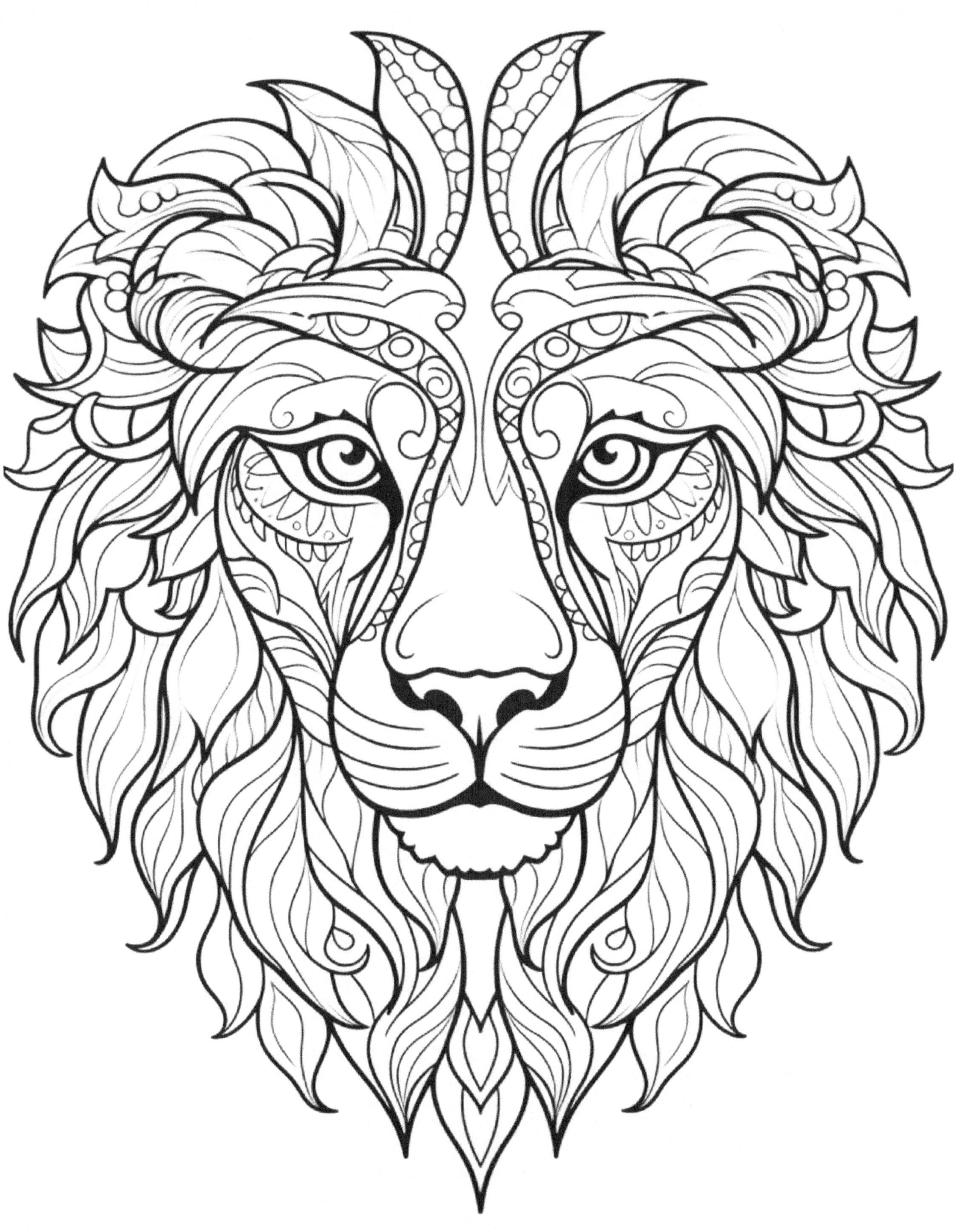

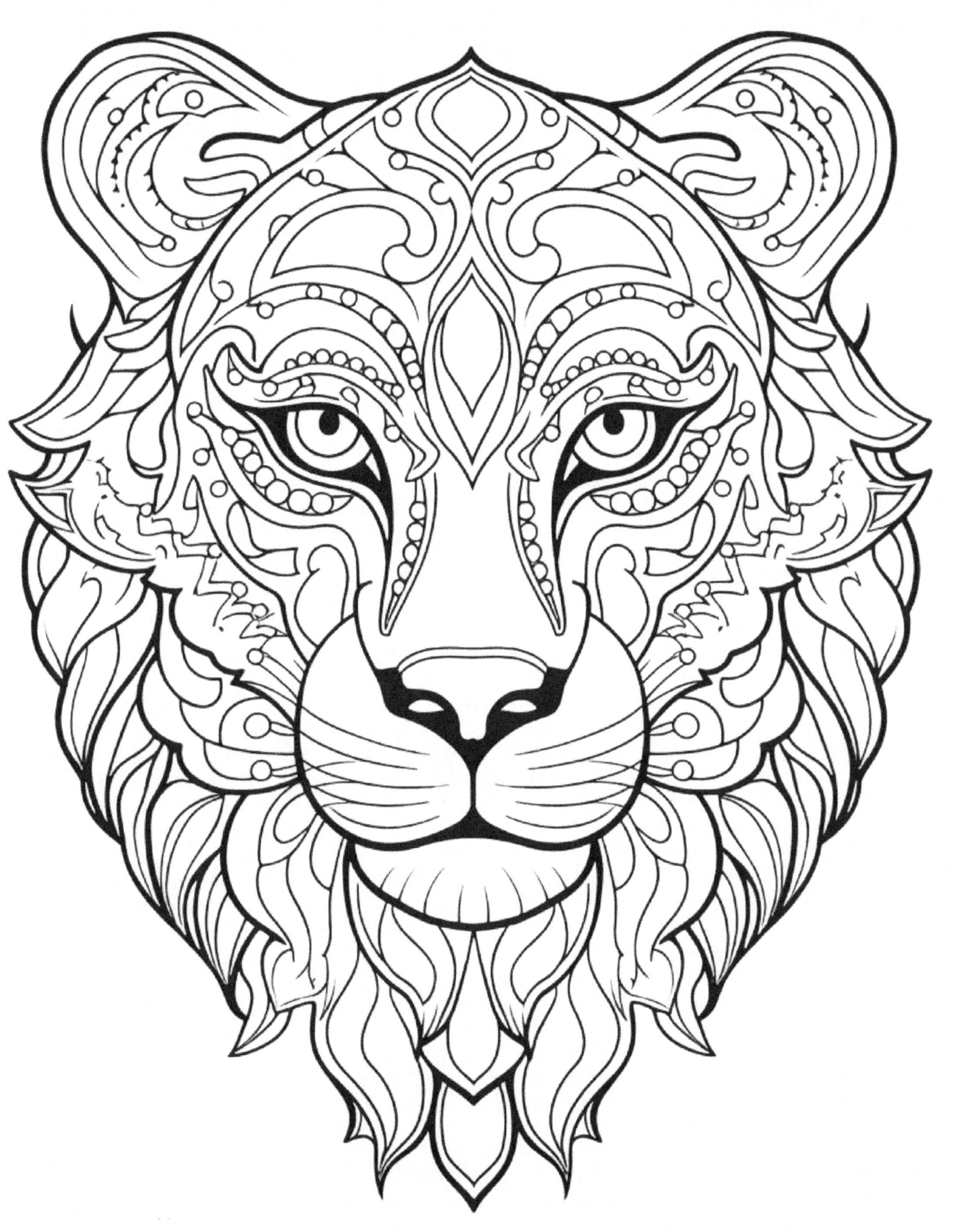

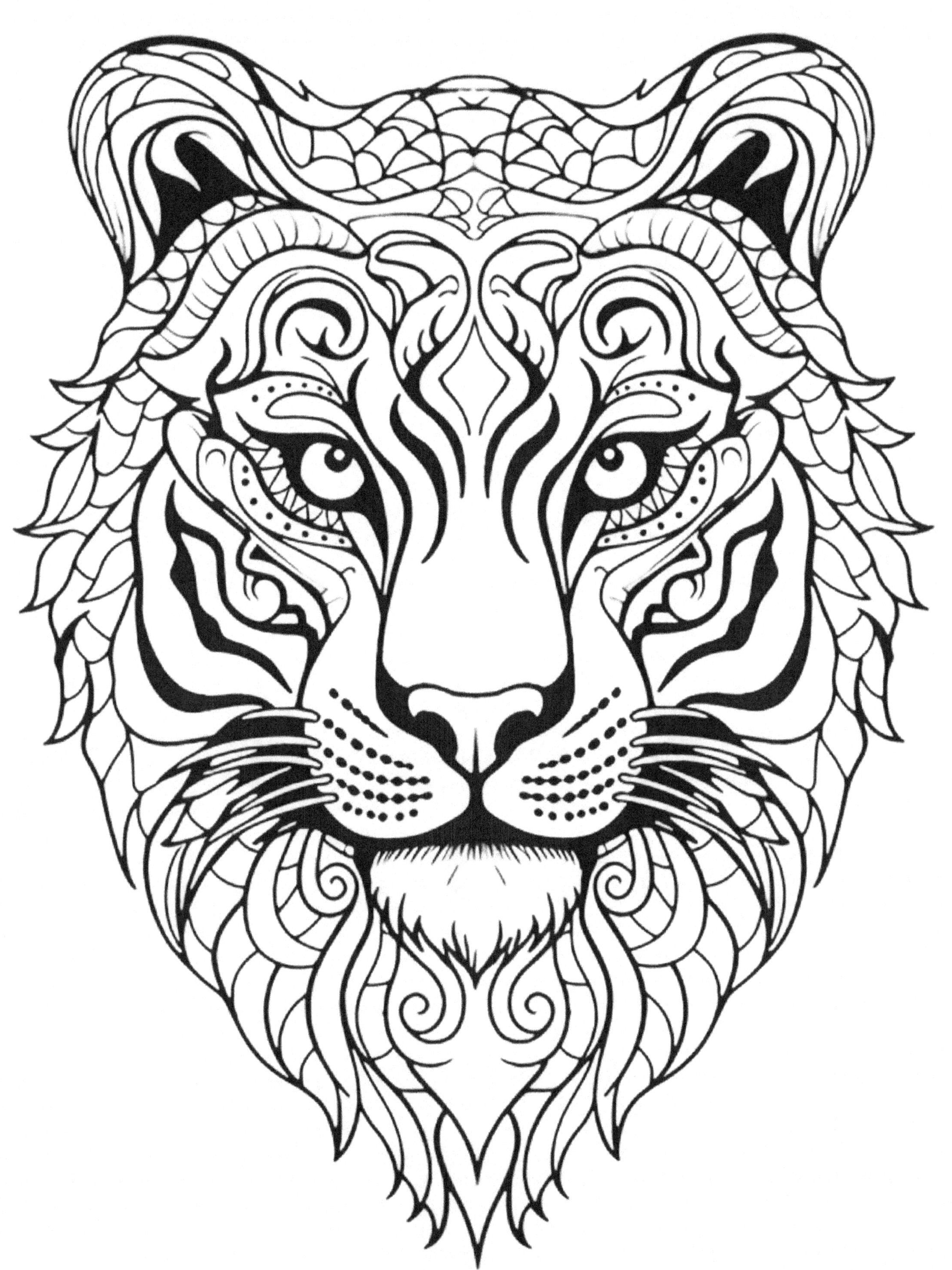

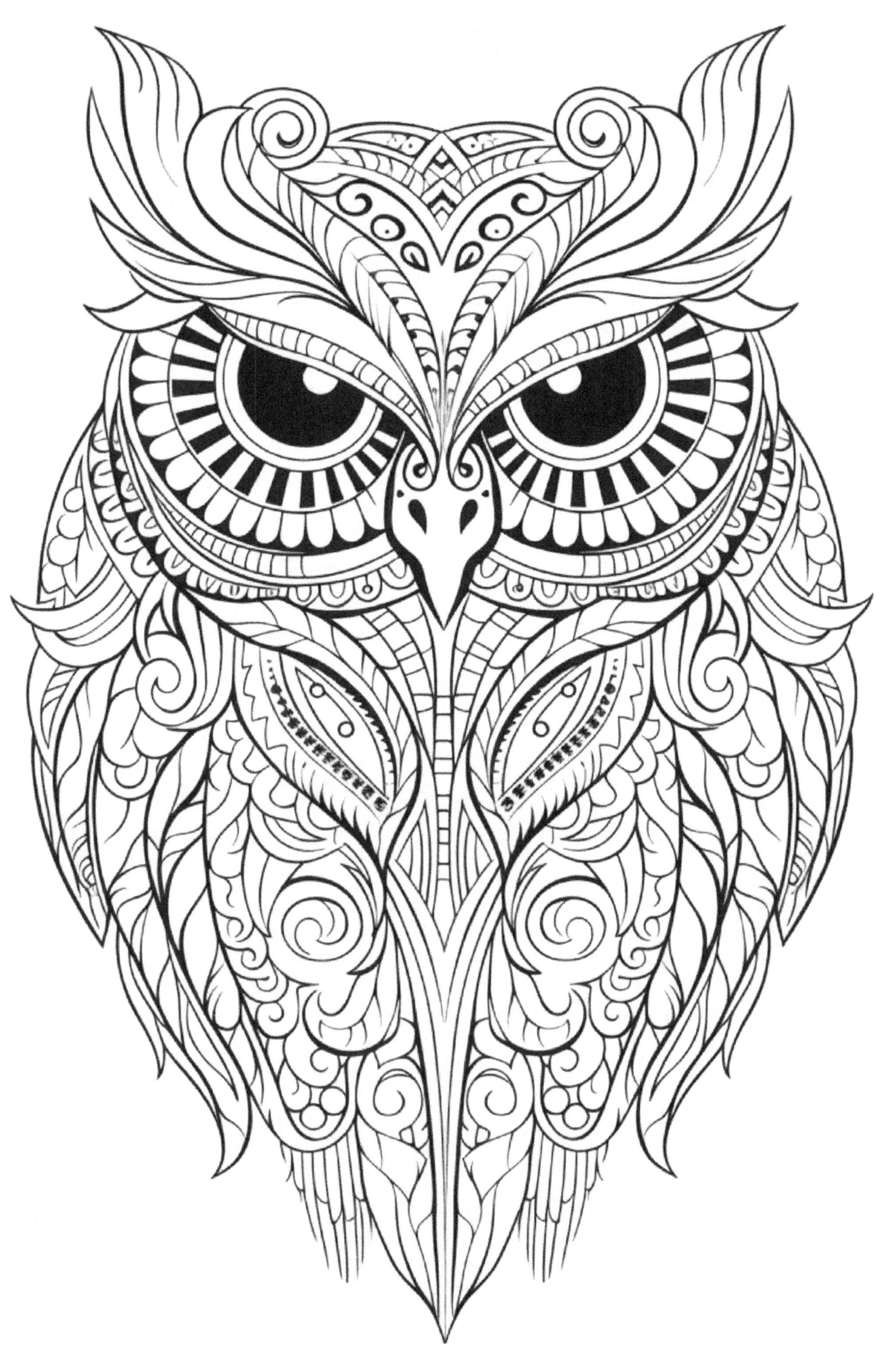

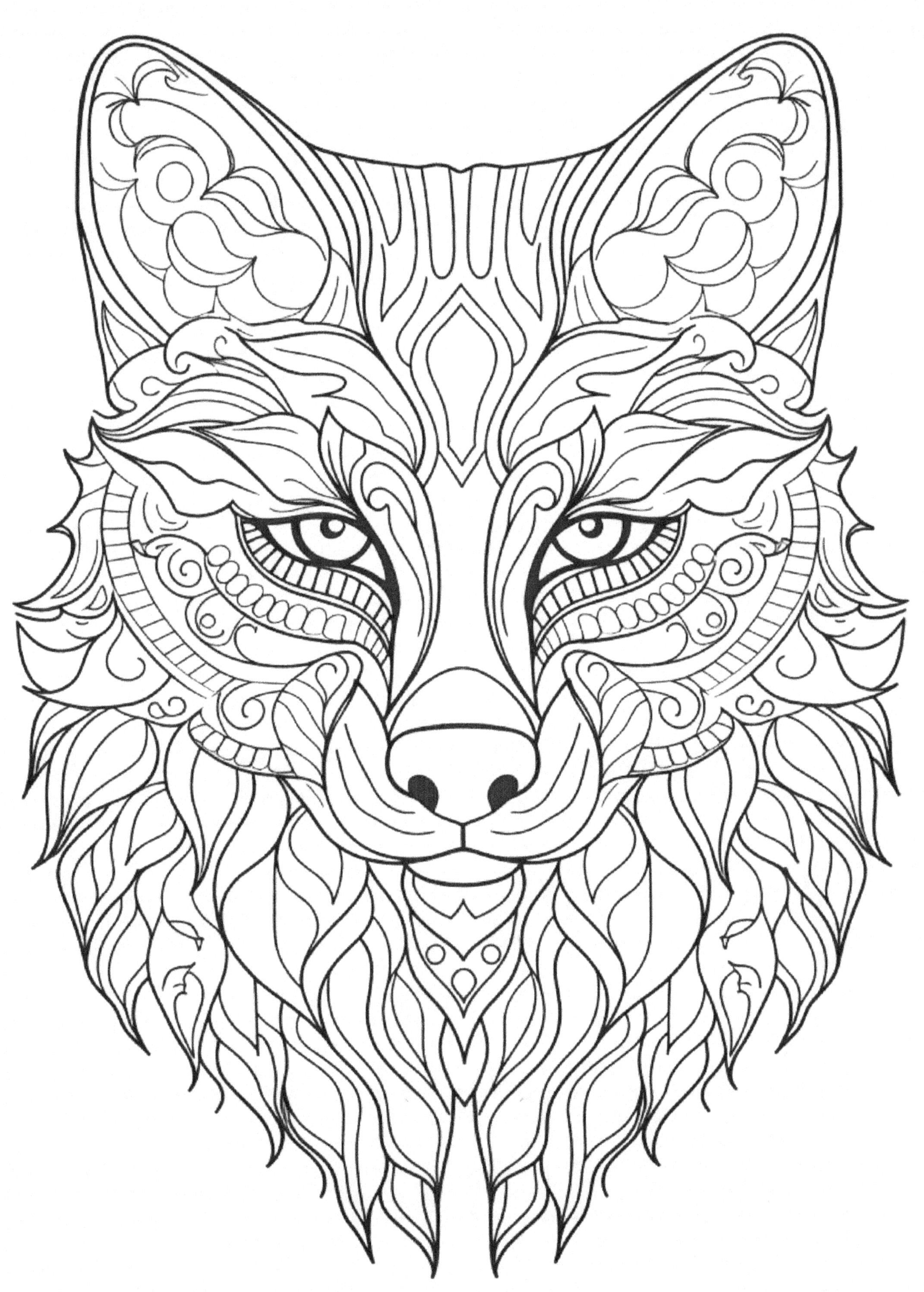

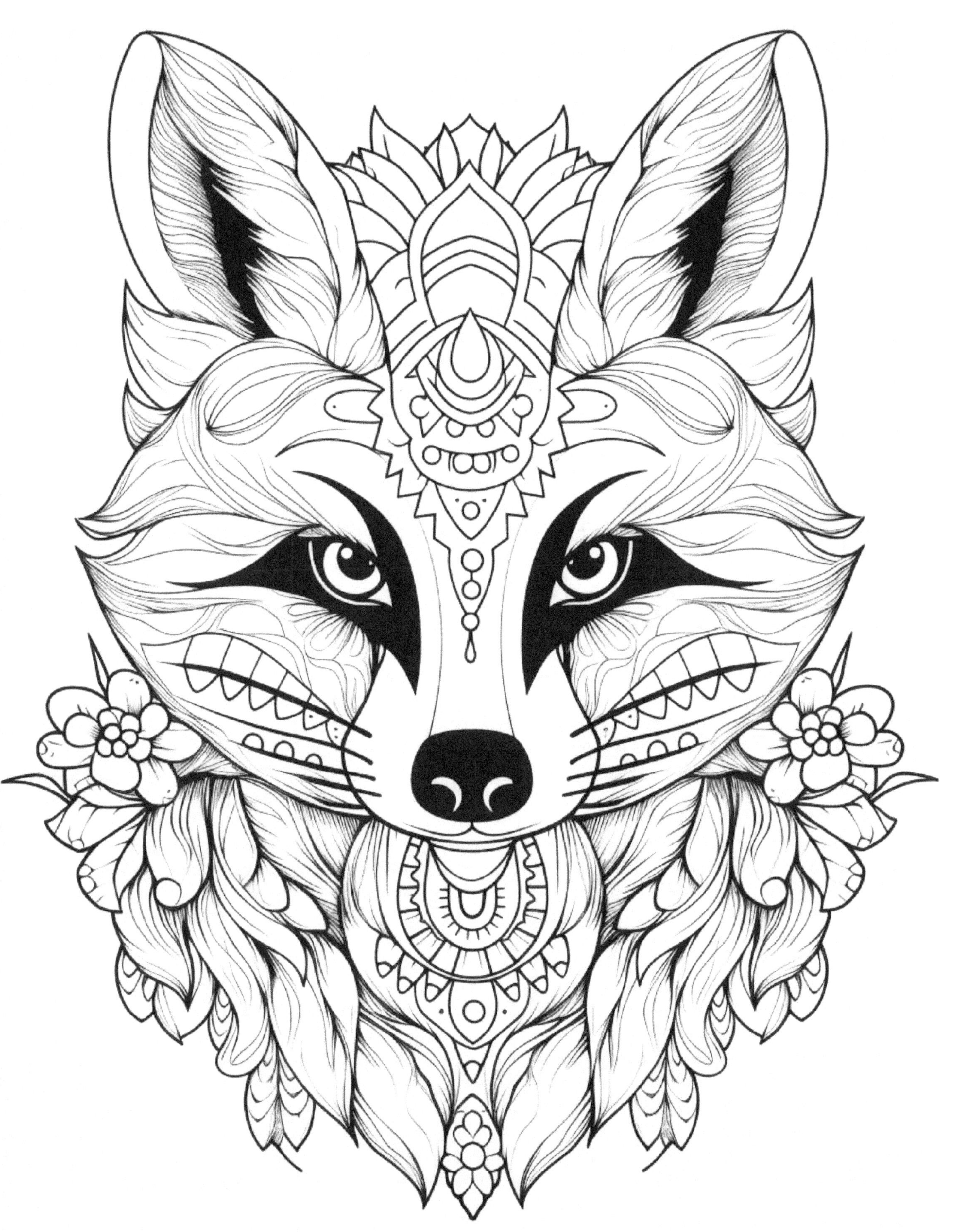

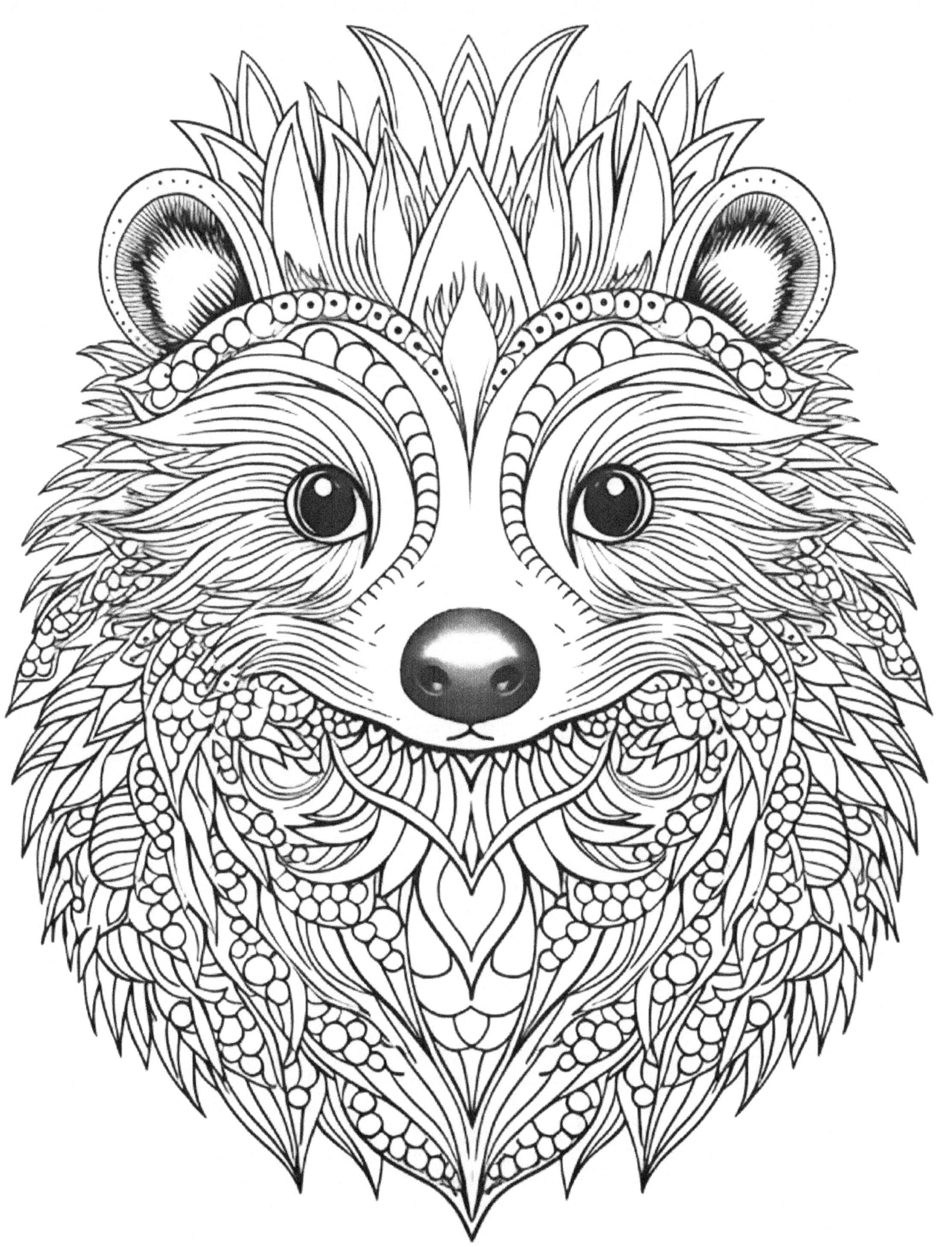

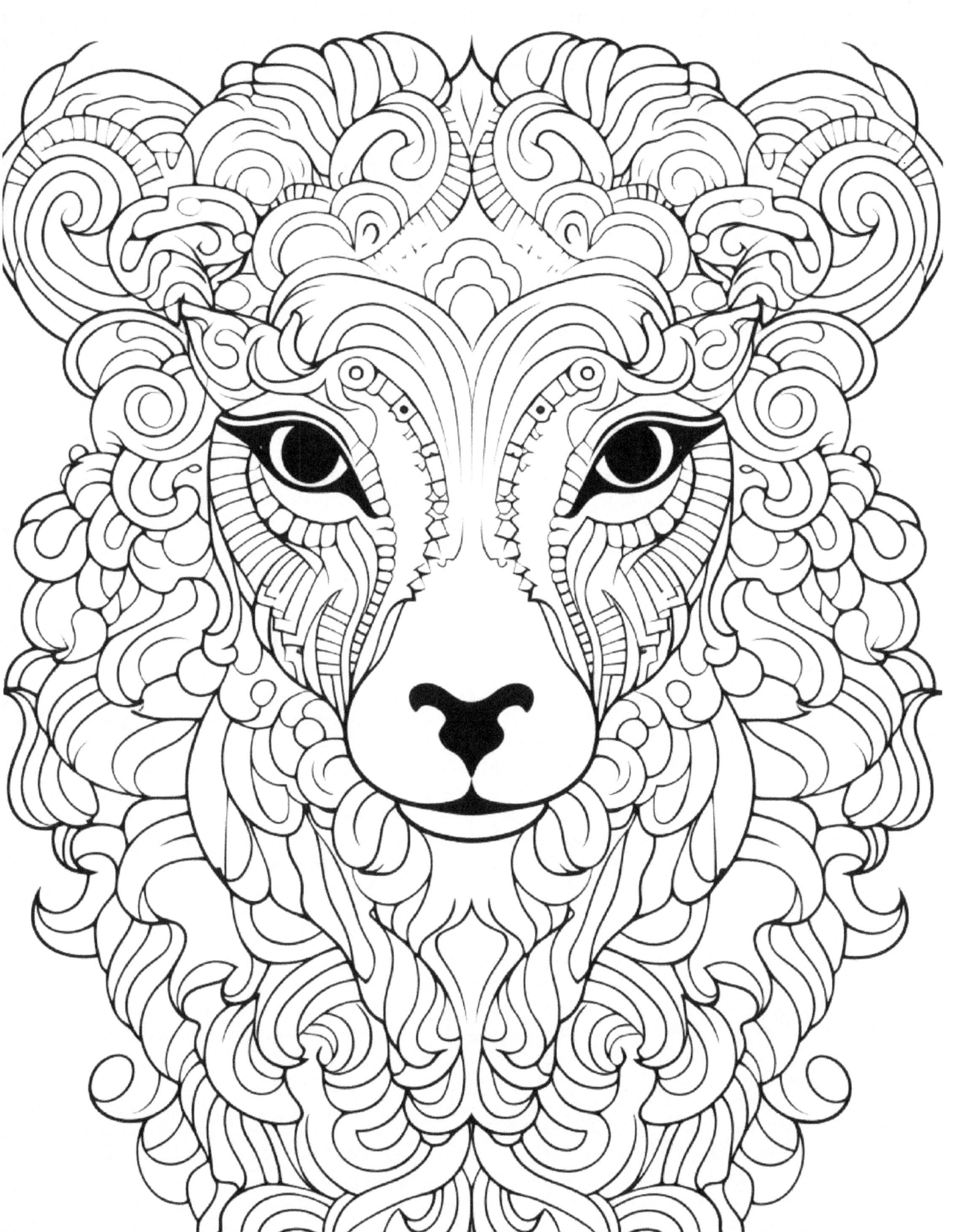

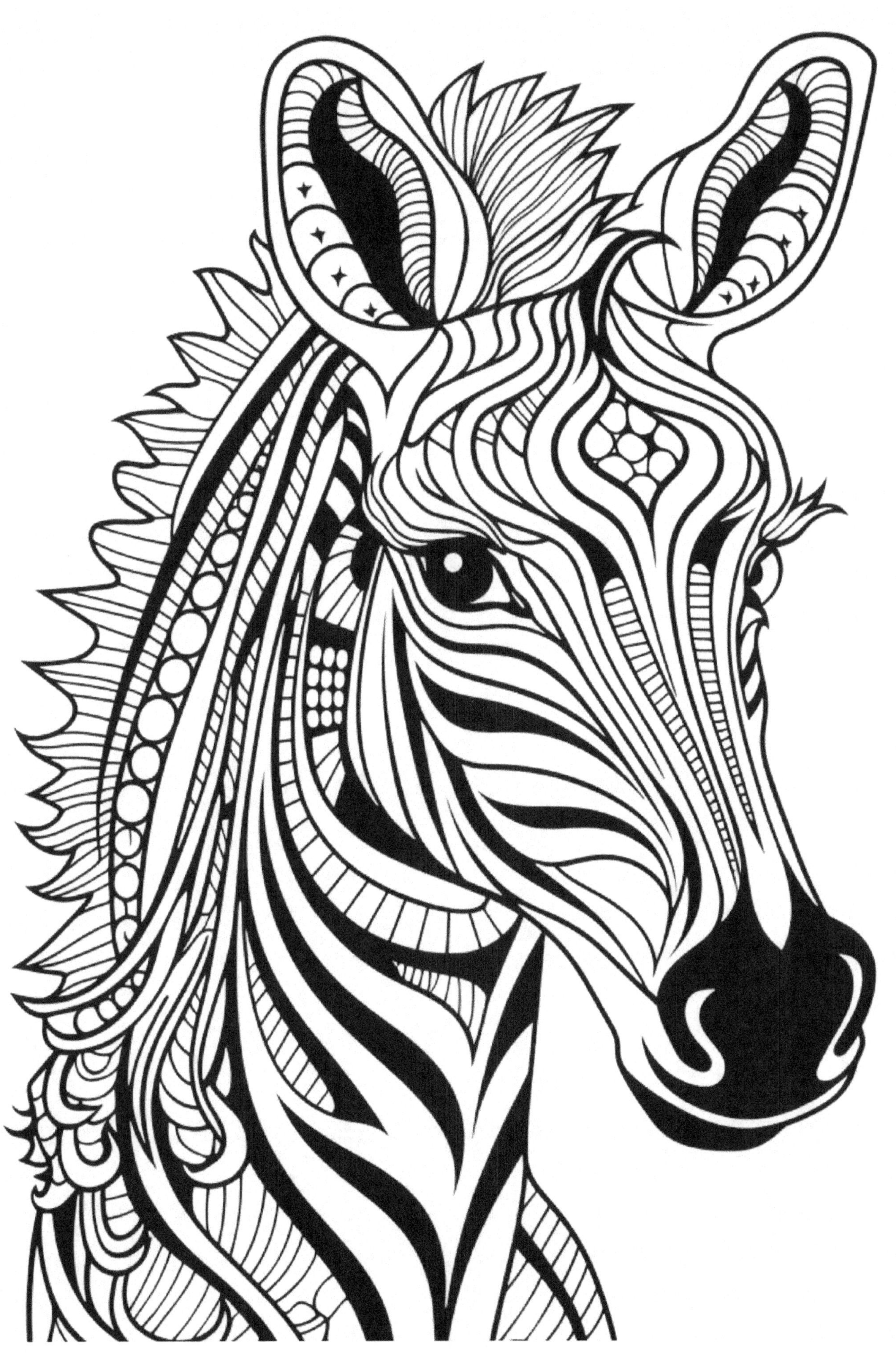

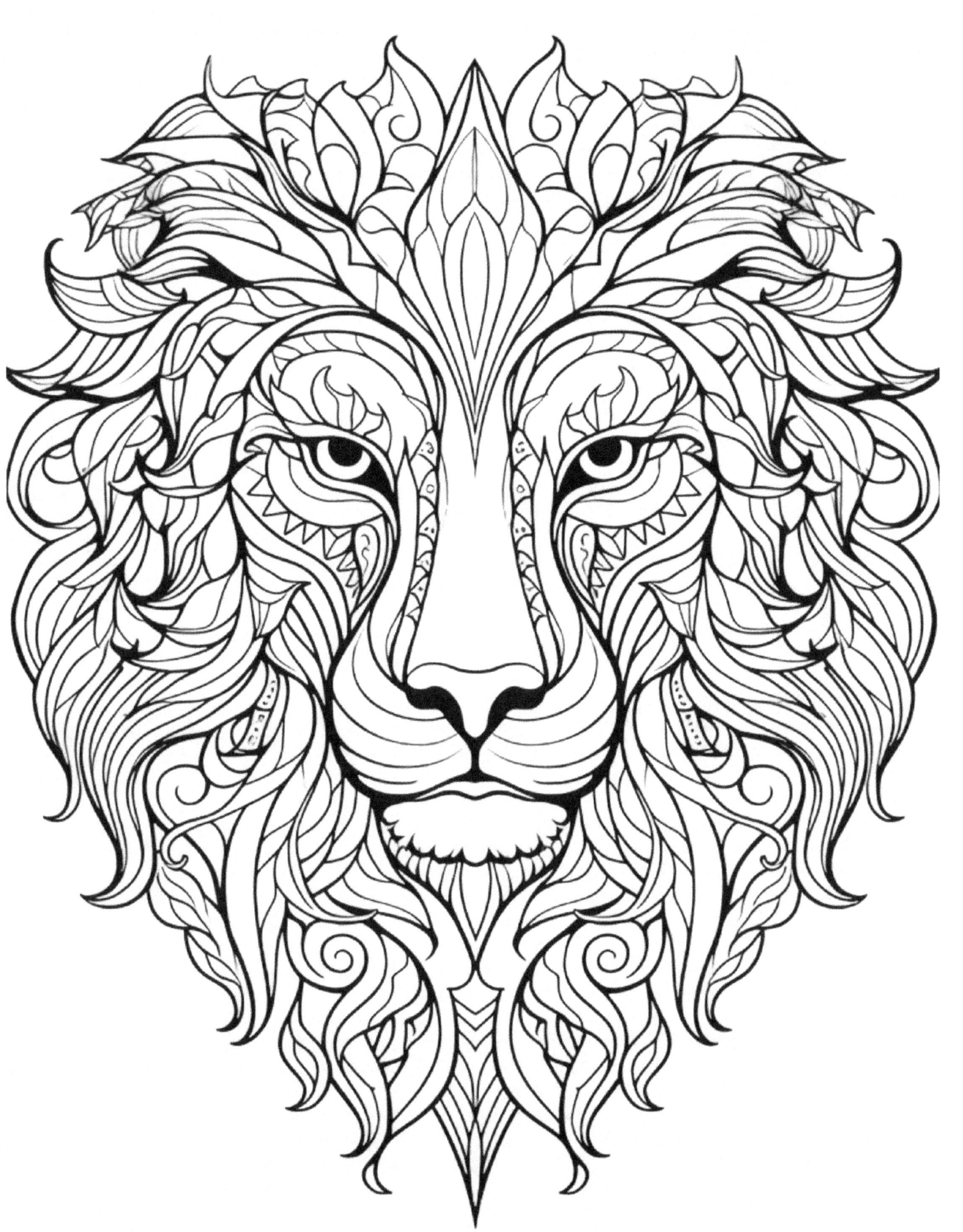

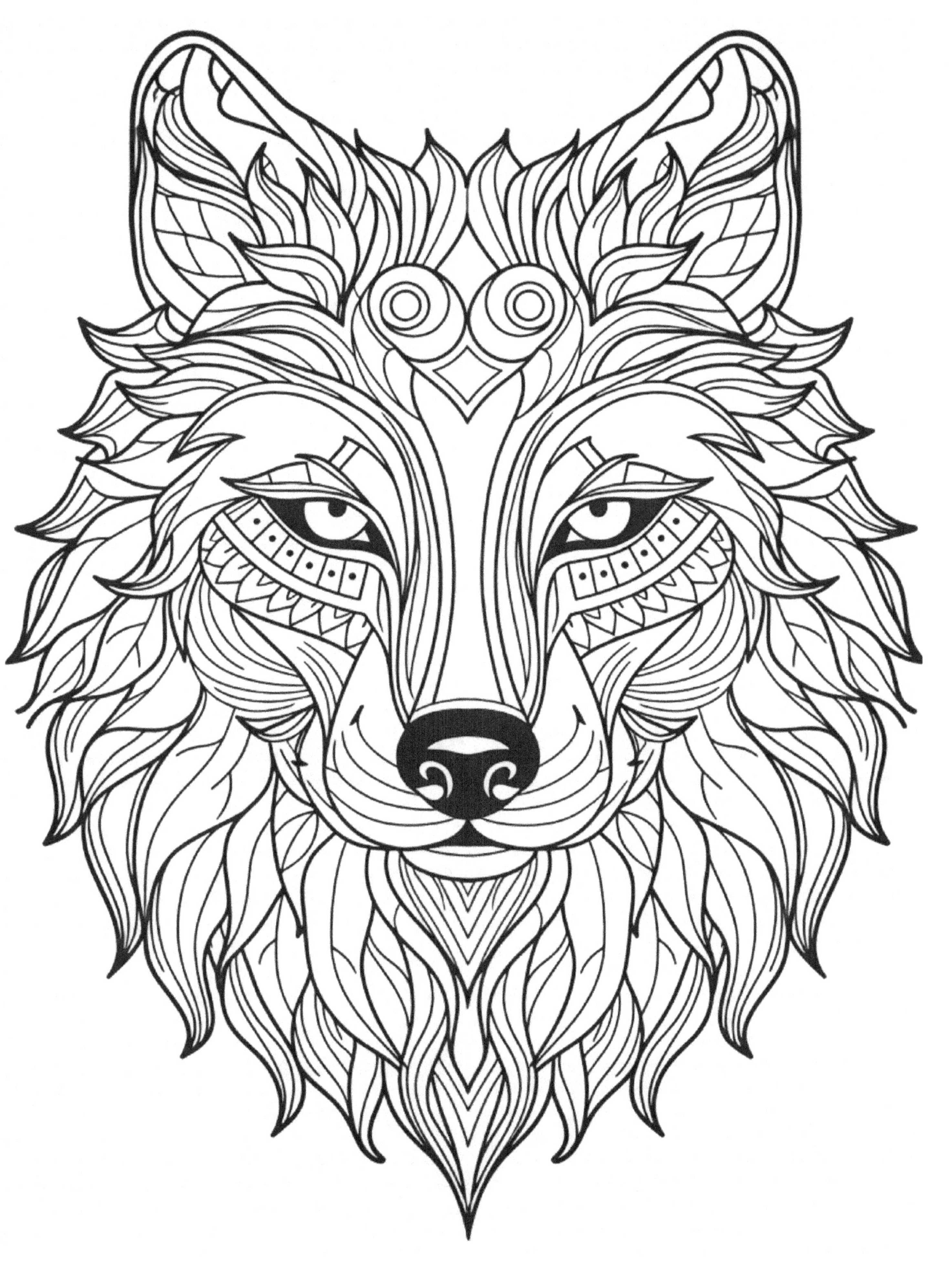

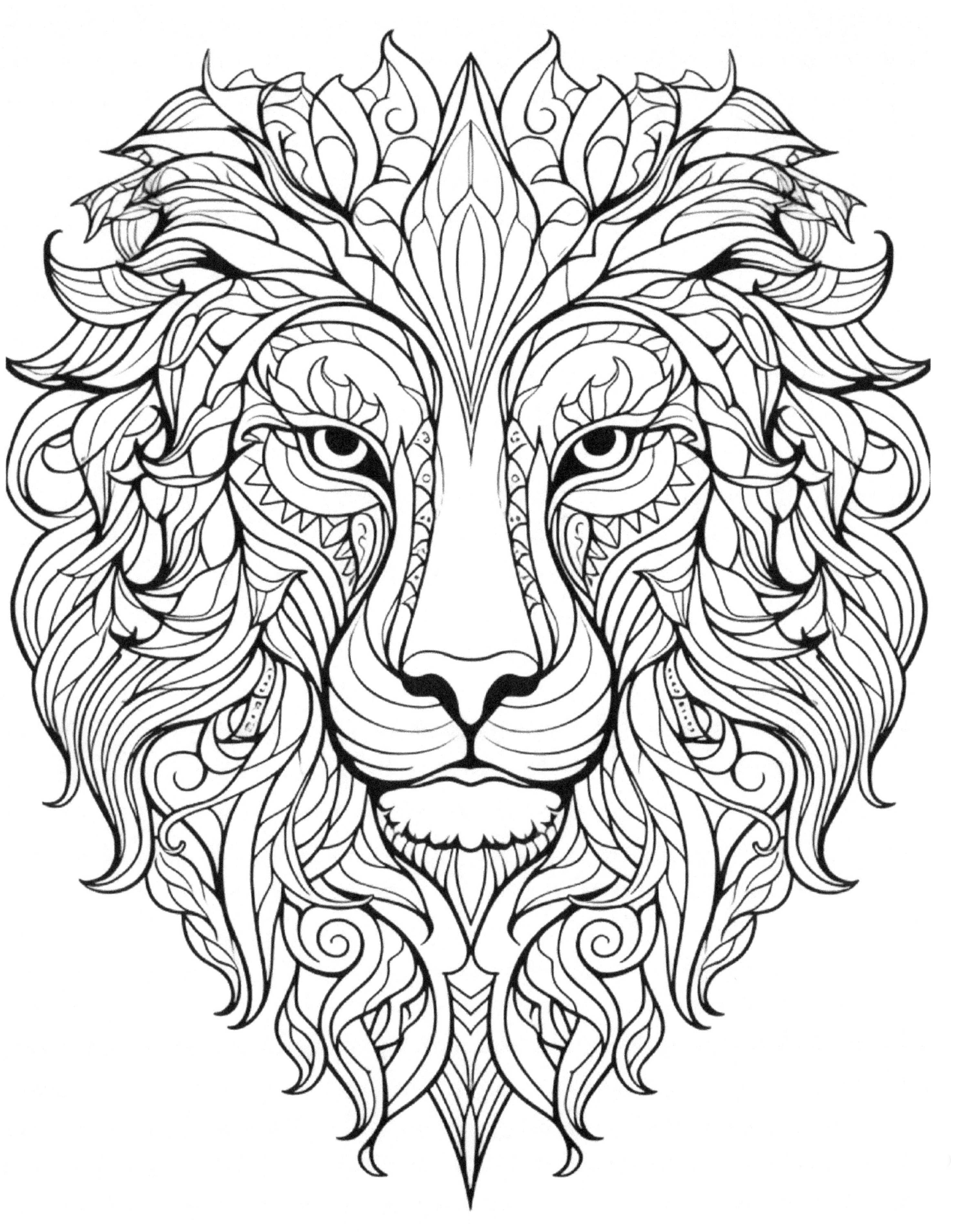

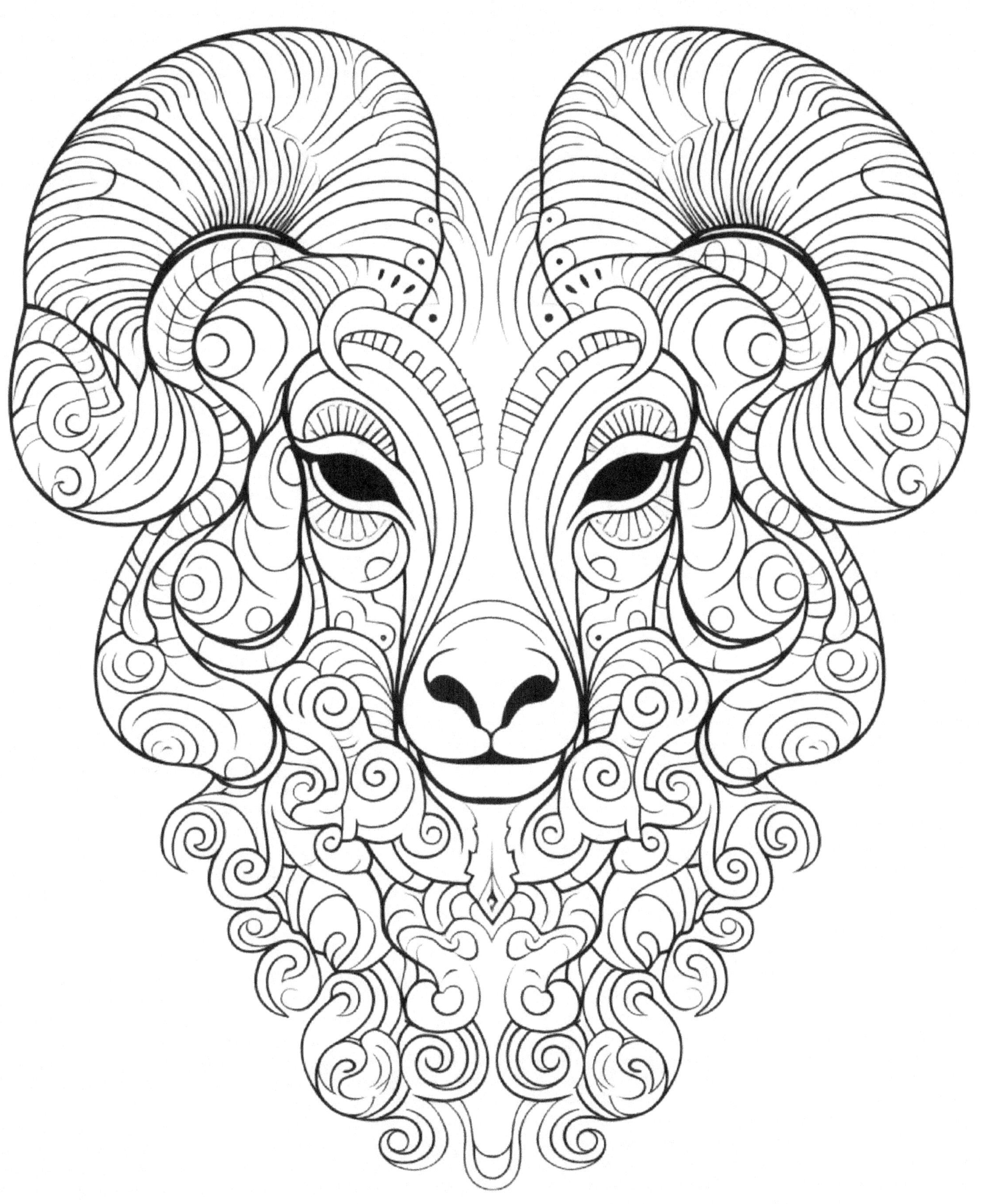

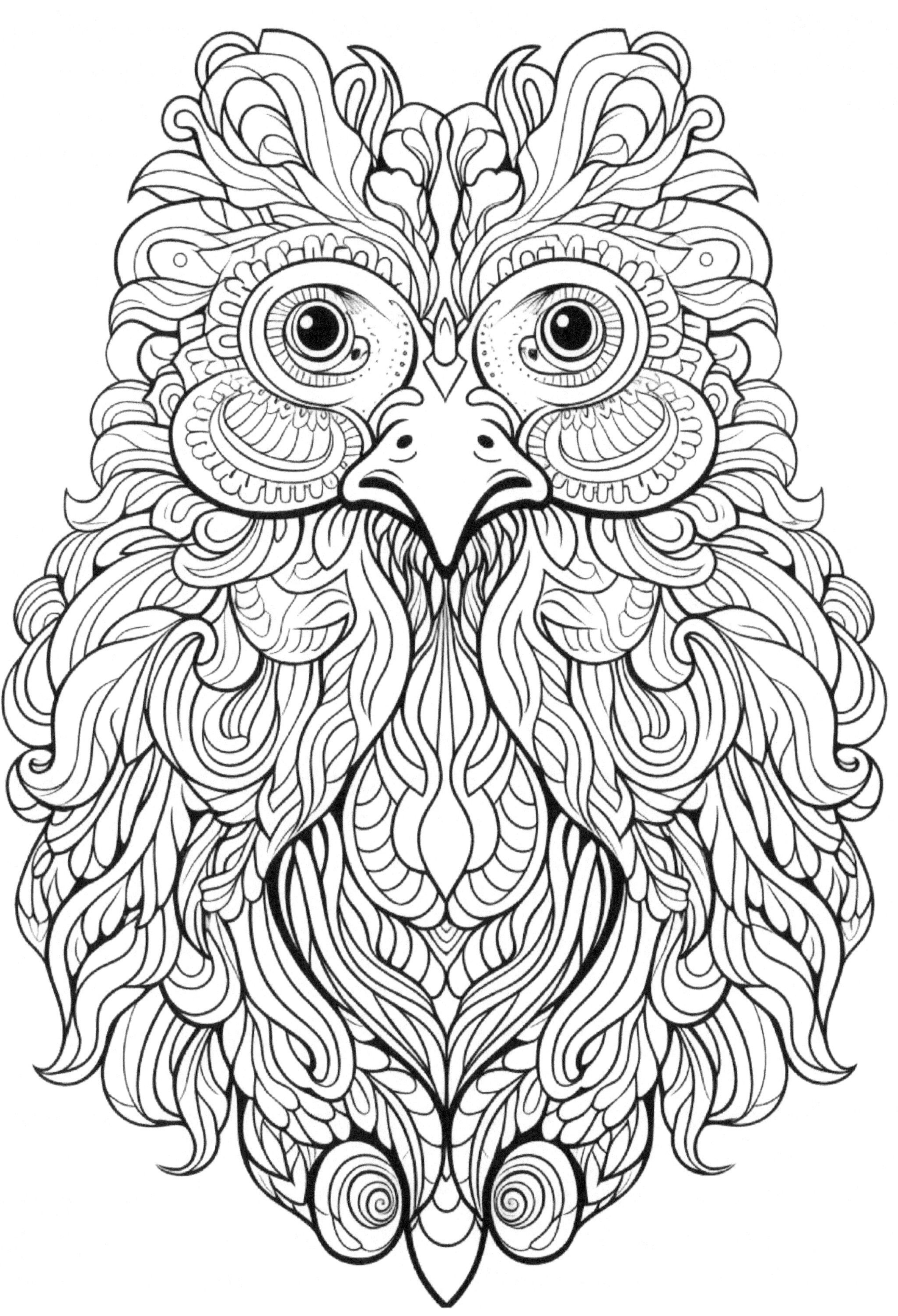

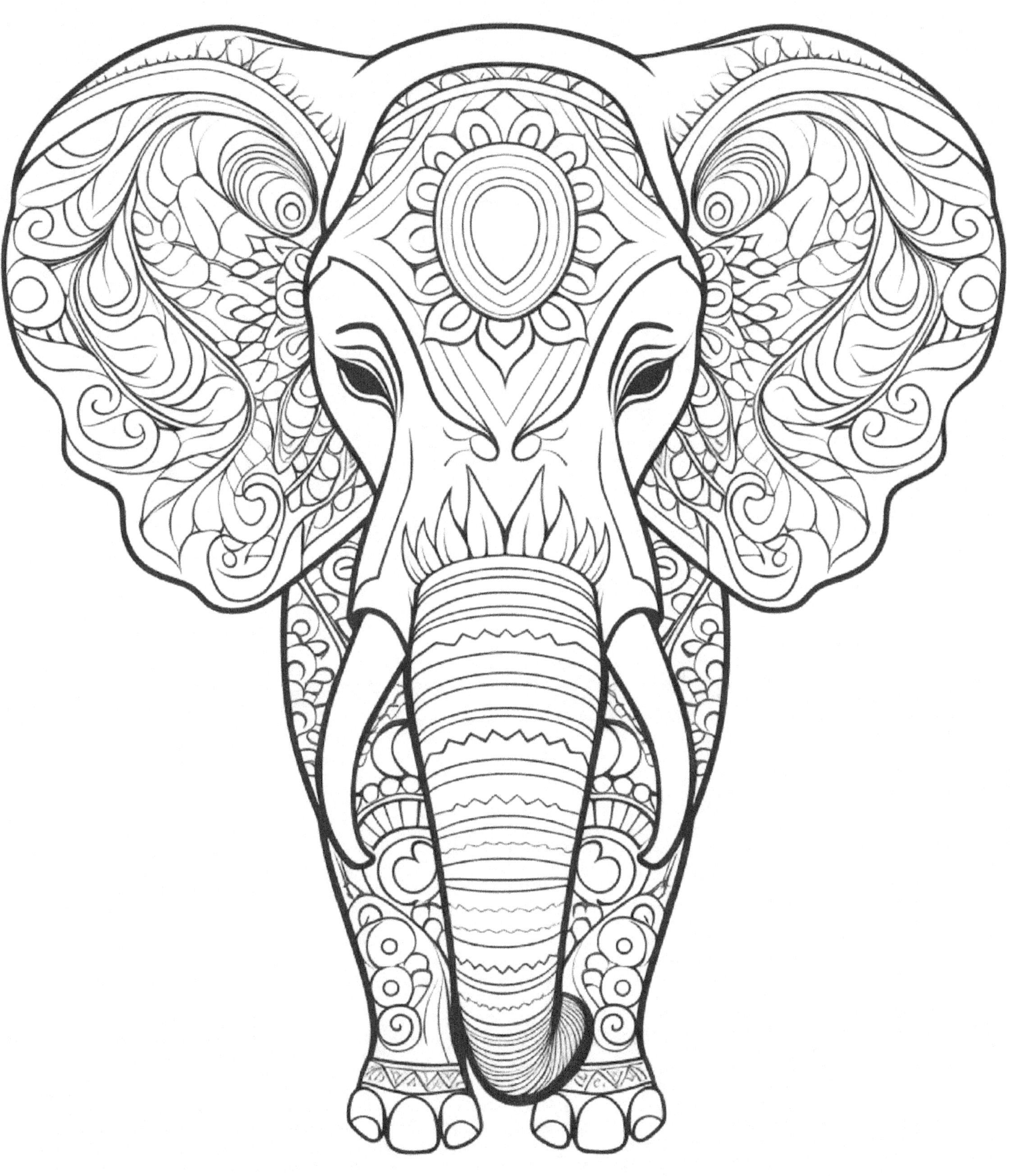

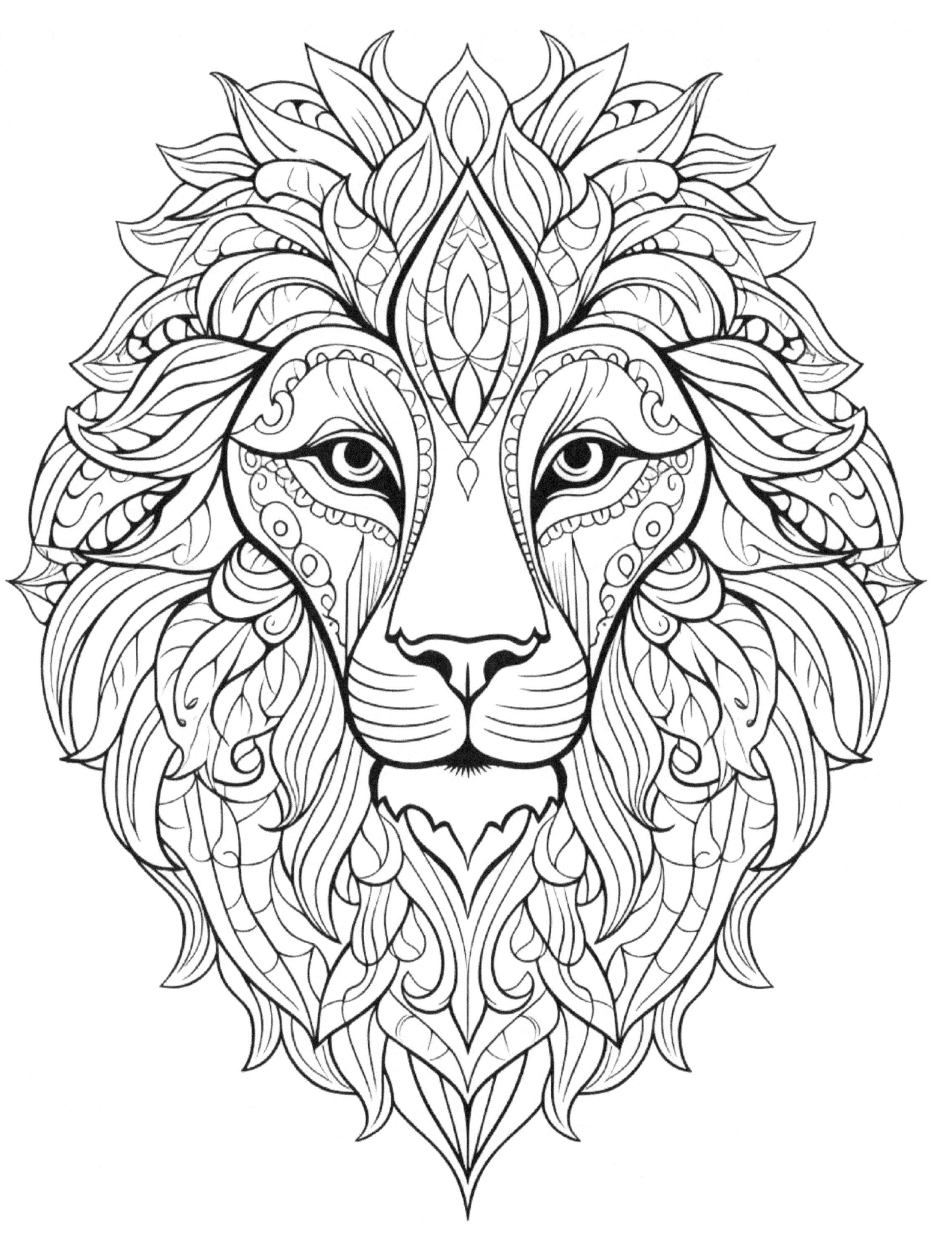

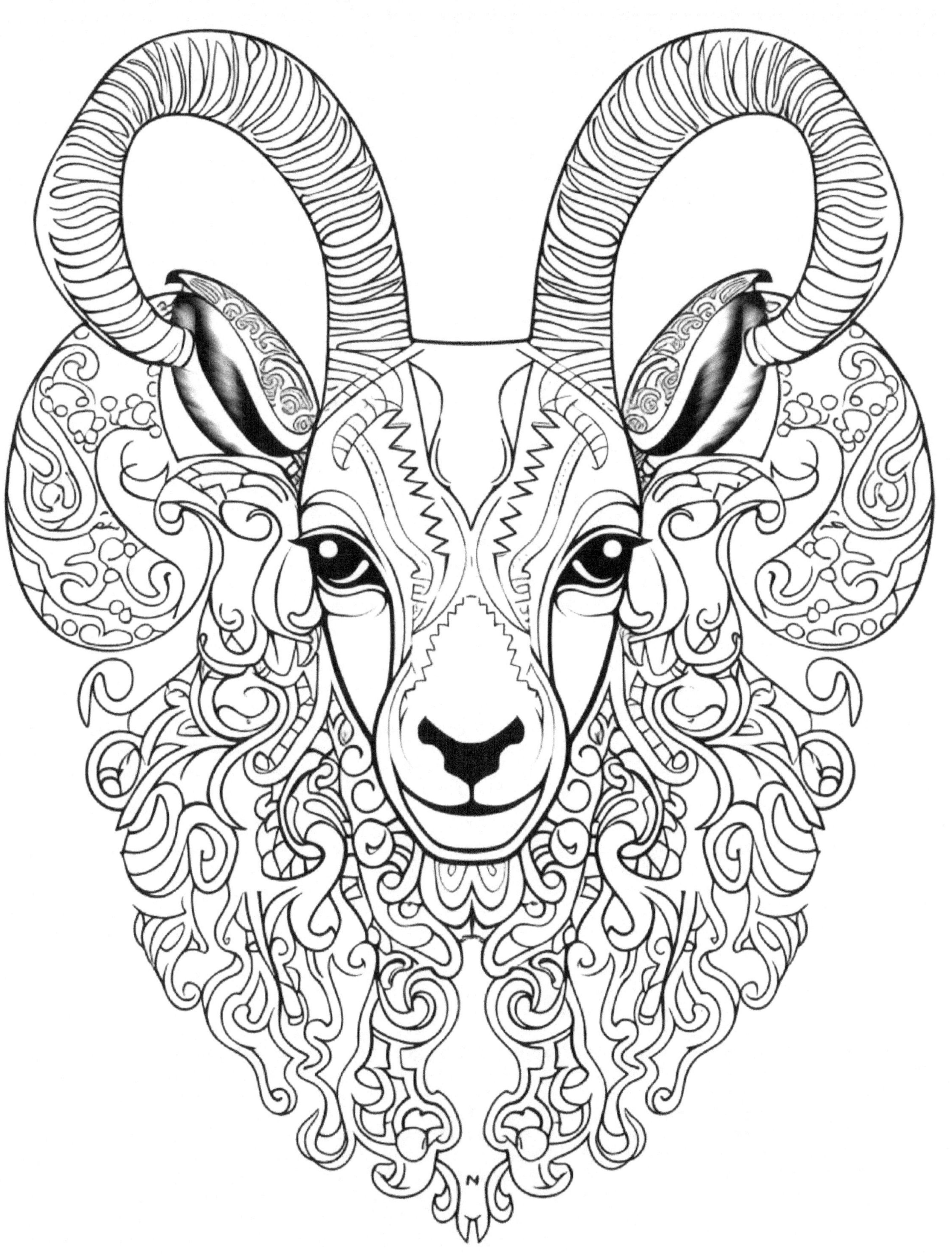

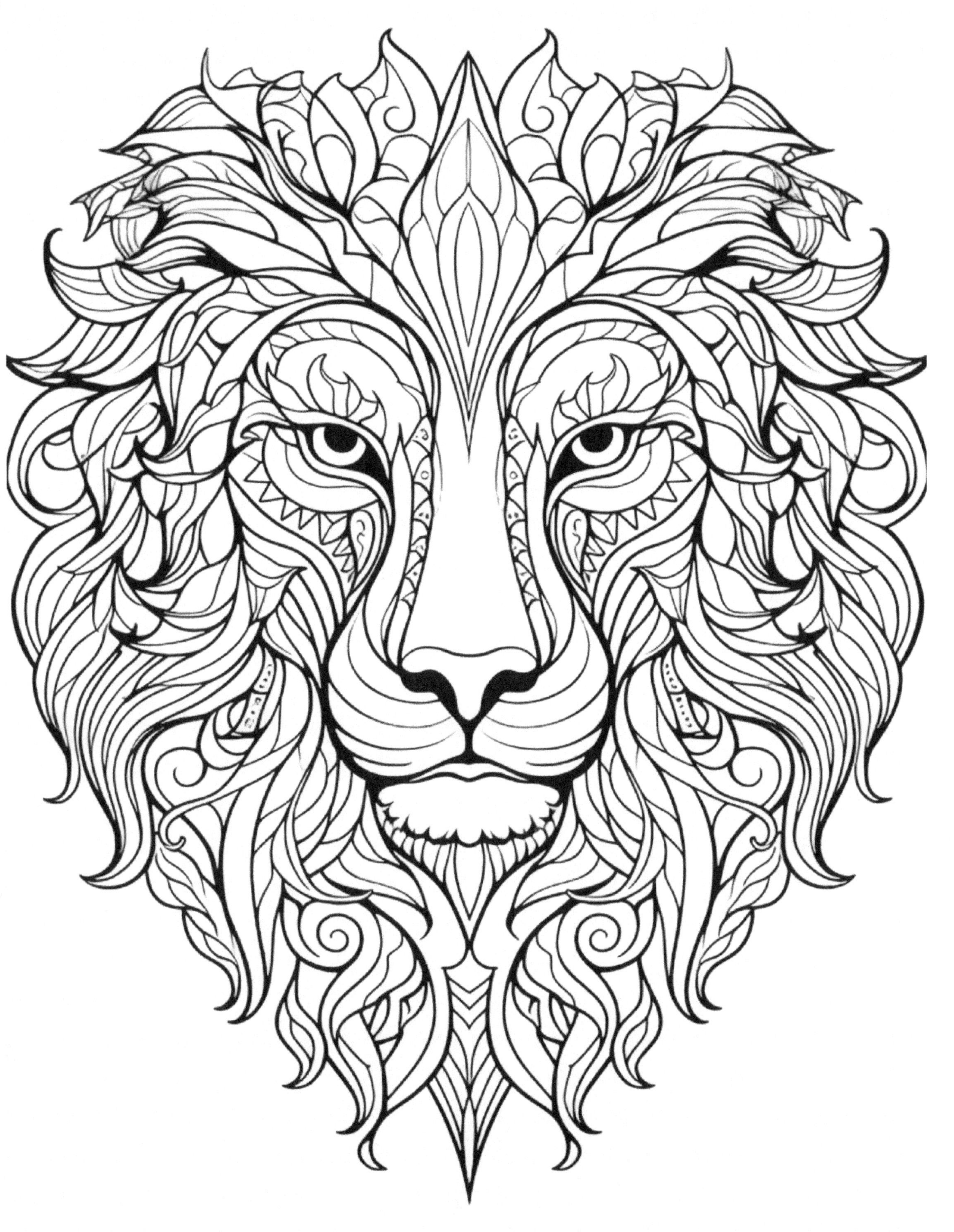